TRUE STORIES
about THE BIBLE

BOOKS

True Stories about the Bible

Copyright © 2005 O Books
An imprint of John Hunt Publishing Ltd., The Bothy, Deershot
Lodge, Park Lane, Ropley, Hants, SO24 0BE, UK
office@johnhunt-publishing.com
www.o-books.net

USA and Canada
NBN
custserv@nbnbooks.com
Tel: 1 800 462 6420 Fax: 1 800 338 4550

Australia
Brumby Books
sales@brumbybooks.com
Tel: 61 3 9761 5535 Fax: 61 3 9761 7095

New Zealand
Peaceful Living
books@peaceful-living.co.nz
Tel: 64 7 57 18105 Fax: 64 7 57 18513

Singapore
STP
davidbuckland@tlp.com.sg
Tel: 65 6276 Fax: 65 6276 7119

South Africa
Alternative Books
altbook@global.co.za
Tel: 27 011 792 7730 Fax: 27 011 972 7787

Design by Andrew Milne Design Ltd

ISBN 1 905047 34 7

A CIP catalogue record for this book is available
from the British Library.

Printed by Maple-Vail Book Manufacturing Group, USA

Contents

— *Part 1* —
TRUE STORIES
about THE BIBLE

The Bounty Bible

The Bounty sets sail

One of the most dramatic examples of the Bible's ability to transform men and women involved the famous mutiny on the Bounty.

In 1787, on the orders of King George III of England, one of His Majesty's transport ships, the Bounty, sailed from Spithead to the islands of the South Sea.

Captain Bligh

The Bounty was captained by Captain Bligh. On board were twenty-five very rough-and-ready sailors who came to hate Captain Bligh because he was such a strict disciplinarian. The plan was to sail to one of the islands in the South Seas, Tahiti, to collect a tropical fruit known as breadfruit, which had white flesh and a bread-like texture. They had orders to dig up some of these breadfruit trees and then take them to Jamaica. There they were to replant the breadfruit trees to increase the food supply for the people of Jamaica.

> **LIGHT from the BIBLE**
>
> *"Your statutes are wonderful;*
> *therefore I obey them.*
> *The unfolding of your words gives light;*
> *it gives understanding to the simple."*
> PSALM 119:129-130

Tahiti

When they landed at Tahiti they thought they were in paradise. They were surrounded by blue seas, golden sands, and glamorous girls. Before long every sailor had his own girlfriend and, to the sailors' delight, they stayed there for several months.

Mutiny on the Bounty

Captain Bligh made himself even more unpopular when he suddenly announced one day that they were going to set sail the next day! Fletcher Christian, one of the officers, complained about this and had secret meetings with the sailors. They talked about a mutiny, about killing Captain Bligh and getting rid of the Bounty. However, the ship did set sail.

But a few days later Fletcher Christian masterminded a mutiny and tied up Bligh. So Captain William Bligh and eighteen men were set adrift in a small boat. After forty-eight hazardous days on the open seas, with sheer determination and superb seamanship, Bligh and his sailors managed to reach a friendly port on the island of Timor. From there they made their way back to England.

Quotation to ponder

"Surrounded by institutionalized brutality, tortured by cold, hunger, untreated illness and deprived of correspondence with family, the women of our small 'political' zone drew strength and support from 2 Bibles, which had passed from one generation of prisoners to another."

IRANA RATUSHINSKAYA,
DESCRIBING HER 4 YEARS IN A
RUSSIAN PRISON

Christian and the mutineers sailed back to Tahiti to collect their girlfriends, who willingly sailed off to sea with them. So the Bounty now set sail with nine mutineers, six Tahitian men, nine women, and a Tahitian girl of 15.

LIGHT *from the* BIBLE

"I open my mouth and pant, longing for your commands. Turn to me and have mercy on me, as you always do to those who love your name. Direct my footsteps according to your word; let no sin rule over me. Redeem me from the oppression of men, that I may obey your precepts. Make your face shine upon your servant and teach me your decrees. Streams of tears flow from my eyes, for your law is not obeyed."

PSALM 119:131-136

Pitcairn Island

They came across Pitcairn Island, a tiny dot in the South Pacific only two miles long and a mile wide. They landed on this uninhabited extinct volcano island with its lush vegetation. They took everything they could from the Bounty, and then they set fire to her.

Paradise on earth?

On Pitcairn Island they looked forward to paradise on earth, but they soon found themselves living in a kind of hell.

One of the mutineers used the old copper kettle from the Bounty to rig up a distillery, and he used tree roots to make spirits. Soon the sailors and women became drunk and remained that way for days, weeks, and even months on end. Some of the men became like animals, fighting among themselves. One committed suicide by flinging himself over the edge of a volcanic cliff. After several years only two men were left, Edward Young and Alexander Smith. Young was an older man, seriously ill with asthma. The women, with the 18 children who had been born to them, seized the guns one night and barricaded themselves in.

Quotation to ponder

"The Bible – banned, burned, beloved. More widely read, more frequently attacked than any other book in history. Generations of intellectuals have attempted to discredit it; dictators of every age have outlawed it and executed those who read it. Yet soldiers carry it into battle believing it more powerful than their weapons. Fragments of it smuggled into solitary prison cells have transformed ruthless killers into gentle saints."

CHARLES COLSON

The two sailors were left to live their lives on their own, and none of the women or children would go near them.

Bounty's Bible

Alexander Smith at last acknowledged the sinfulness of his life, and became concerned about the future of those who looked to him for leadership. He began to think seriously of God.

Young realized that he was dying. One day he went along to the ship's chest and rummaged around in it.

At the bottom, among a pile of old papers, he found an old, leather-bound, worm-eaten, mildewed book. It was the Bounty's Bible. He had not read anything for years. He started to read at the beginning of Genesis. He also taught his friend Lex to read. These two wrecks of humanity read the Bible together for many hours each day.

> **LIGHT** *from the* **BIBLE**
>
> *"Your word is a lamp to my feet and a light for my path. I have taken an oath and confirmed it, that I will follow your righteous laws. I have suffered much; preserve my life, O LORD , according to your word."*
>
> PSALM 119:105-107

The children return

Edward Young and Alexander Smith prayed, as best they could. They sought light and guidance for all they were worth from the pages of the Old Testament.

The little children were the first to come back as they noticed the change in the men. Then the women came back, and they sat around in a circle while Edward, and sometimes Lex, read to them. When they came to the Psalms they realized that they were hymns, and so in their own very strange way they started to sing the Psalms together. Edward died peacefully in his sleep one night.

"Working like a mole"
Lex kept on reading the Bible. When he came to the New Testament he said, "I had been working like a mole for years, and suddenly it was as if the doors were flung wide open, and I saw the light, and I met God in Jesus Christ. And the burden of my sin rolled away, and I found new life in Christ."

Quotation to ponder

"The most learned, acute, and diligent student cannot, in the longest life, obtain an entire knowledge of this one Volume. The more deeply he works the Mine, the richer and more abundant he finds the Ore; new Light continually beams from this Source of Heavenly knowledge, to direct the conduct, and illustrate the work of God and the ways of men; and he will at last leave the Work confessing, that the more he studied the Scriptures, the fuller conviction he has of his own ignorance, and of their inestimable value!"
WALTER SCOTT

LIGHT *from the* BIBLE

"Accept, O LORD, the willing praise of my mouth,
and teach me your laws.
Though I constantly take my life in my hands,
I will not forget your law.
The wicked have set a snare for me,
but I have not strayed from your precepts.
Your statutes are my heritage forever;
they are the joy of my heart.
My heart is set on keeping your decrees
to the very end."

PSALM 119:108-112

A boat from Boston

After they had been on Pitcairn Island for 18 years, a boat
from Boston came across the island, and the captain
landed. He found a quiet, godly community, characterized
by a grace and a peace that he had never before seen.

Their leader greeted the captain: "I am Alexander
Smith. I am the only survivor from the Bounty. If you
want to arrest me, you can."
The captain replied, "I don't know anything about the
Bounty, but what I do know is that these people here
clearly need you."

Before he left the island Lex told him every detail
about the last 18 years of his life. When the captain
returned to the United States he reported that in all his
travels he had never met another group of people who
were so good and so loving. He knew that there was
only one book which could produce a miracle like that.

Quotation to ponder

"I know not a better rule of reading the Scripture,
than to read it through from beginning to end and,
when we have finished it once, to begin it again. We
shall meet with many passages which we can make
little improvement of, but not so many in the second
reading as in the first, and fewer in the third than in
the second: provided we pray to him who has the keys
to open our understandings, and to anoint our eyes
with his spiritual ointment."

JOHN NEWTON

Mary Jones and her Bible

Mary's longing for a Bible

A s Mary and her mother were walking home from a church service Mary reflected on the preacher's words from Psalm 119, "God's Word is a lamp to my feet and a light unto my path." Mary longed for a Bible of her own so that she could learn more of God's Word!

> **LIGHT** *from the* **BIBLE**
>
> *"Thy word is a lamp unto my feet, and a light unto my path."*
>
> PSALM 119:105 KJV

Llanfihangely Pennant

Mary Jones was born on 16 December 1784 in the Welsh village of Llanfihangely Pennant. Her father had been a weaver, but he died when Mary was four. Mary and her mother had very little money.

Long walk to school

When Mary was eight years old, a school opened about an hour's walk from Llanfihangel. Mary walked to and from school, a two-hour round-trip, each day. In 1794 the ten-year-old Mary became the first in her family to learn to read. Her accomplishment was rewarded when her teacher invited her to read aloud from the Welsh Bible at school. Mary was so moved by the words she was reading she resolved then and there to do everything in her power to own a Bible. However, her mother could not afford to buy her a Bible. But one of her neighbors did have a Bible. So every Saturday afternoon Mary went to Mrs. Evans' house and there read her Bible for hours on end.

Doing chores

One day as Mary was washing her family's clothes in the river when she had an idea. She could earn some money by washing clothes for other people and so save enough money for a Bible of her own.

When Mrs. Evans heard of Mary's plan, she gave Mary some chicks. When the chicks became hens, Mary sold their eggs.

Mary soon found other ways for earning money: she looked after children, weeded gardens, knitted woolen socks, tended a bee hive, and worked alongside farm hands during harvest.

Quotation to ponder

"I have myself, for many years, made it a practice to read through the Bible once every year. My custom is, to read four or five chapters every morning, immediately after rising from my bed. It employs about an hour of my time, and seems to me the most suitable manner of beginning the day."

JOHN QUINCY ADAMS,
SIXTH PRESIDENT OF THE UNITED STATES

LIGHT *from the* BIBLE

"Now an angel of the Lord said to Philip, 'Go south to the road – the desert road – that goes down from Jerusalem to Gaza.' So he started out, and on his way he met an Ethiopian eunuch, an important official in charge of all the treasury of Candace, queen of the Ethiopians. This man had gone to Jerusalem to worship, and on his way home was sitting in his chariot reading the book of Isaiah the prophet. The Spirit told Philip, 'Go to that chariot and stay near it.'
Then Philip ran up to the chariot and heard the man reading Isaiah the prophet. 'Do you understand what you are reading?' Philip asked. 'How can I,' he said, 'unless someone explains it to me?' So he invited Philip to come up and sit with him."

ACTS 8:26-31

Six years of saving

After saving up for six years Mary finally had enough money to buy a Bible. But in her village there were no Bibles for sale. However Mary knew that a Methodist minister, Thomas Charles, had Bibles for sale in Bala. Bala was over twenty-five miles away. Undaunted, the fifteen-year-old Mary set off alone in 1880 with her money for Bala. Mary walked bare-footed, to save wearing out her shoes. When she arrived in Bala she could not believe her ears. Thomas Charles told her that he had only one Bible left but the he had already been promised to someone else. Mary burst into tears.

Thomas Charles is moved

But when Thomas Charles heard Mary's story he

made her take his last Bible and asked the other person to wait.

Thomas Charles was deeply moved by Mary's hard work and persistence to obtain a Bible. As many people in Wales and throughout Britain were becoming Christians Thomas Charles was all too aware that Bibles should be more readily available. In December 1802, Thomas Charles went to London to a meeting of the committee of the Religious Tract Society. He spoke about the desperate need for Bibles in the Welsh language.

Charles told the committee about Mary Jones' story. Although the committee appreciated the need for Bible distribution, they did not feel that they themselves could meet this need. So a Rev. Joseph Hughes

Quotation to ponder

"A day much to be remembered by me as long a I live. I had such a view of Christ as our High priest, of His love, compassion, power and all-sufficiency, as filled my soul with astonishment, with joy unspeakable and full of glory. My mind was overwhelmed. The truths exhibited to my view appeared too wonderfully gracious to be believed. I could not believe for very Joy."

THOMAS CHARLES, RECALLING 20 JANUARY 1773
WHEN HE HEARD DANIEL ROWLAND PREACH IN HIS
REMOTE CHURCH AT LLANGEITHO IN SOUTH WALES
ON HEBREWS 4:15.

suggested that "a society might be formed for this purpose." It would distribute the Bible in Wales, and, "why not for the United Kingdom; why not for the whole world?"

The founding of the British and Foreign Bible Society

So just over a year later, on 7 March 1804, the British and Foreign Bible Society was born "for the wider distribution of the Scriptures, without note or comment." The BFBS undertook to distribute Bibles throughout the world.

> ### LIGHT *from the* BIBLE
>
> *"As the rain and the snow come down from heaven, and do not return to it without watering the earth and making it bud and flourish, so that it yields seed for the sower and bread for the eater, so is my word that goes out from my mouth: It will not return to me empty, but will accomplish what I desire and achieve the purpose for which I sent it."*
>
> ISAIAH 55:10-11

Worldwide Bible distribution

Similar Bible societies were formed in Germany, the Netherlands, Denmark, Russia, France, Greece, and the USA The Bible Societies worked closely with the growing missionary enterprises and those engaged in Bible translation work. All of the great missionaries, including William Carey in India, Robert Morris in China, Henry Martyn in India, and Adoniram Judson in

Burma, relied on the Bible Societies for support.

By 1907, the BFBS had distributed 203,931,768 Bibles, Testaments, and portions of Scripture throughout the world.

The American Bible Society

The BFBS is now known as the Bible Society. In 2000-2001, the Bible Society in the United Kingdom distributed 149,327 Bibles and 9,333 copies of the New Testament.

The American Bible Society (ABS), founded in 1816, publishes, distributes, and translates the Bible. In 2000-2001, ABS distributed 4,113,106 Bibles and 8,322,112 copies of the New Testament.

Bee-keeping

In her old age, Mary Jones kept bees, sold the honey she collected, and gave the money to the Bible Society. She died at the age of 82. In her hometown of Llanfihangel, a monument to her bears the following inscription, in both English and Welsh:

> "To the remembrance of Mary Jones, who in 1800 at the age of 16, walked from here to Bala, in order to buy a Bible from Rev. Charles in the Welsh language. This event was the cause of the foundation of the British and Foreign Bible Society."

— *Part 2* —
STORIES *illustrating*
BIBLE VIRTUES

Kindness of a stranger

Frozen with cold

On a bitterly cold evening in northern Virginia many years ago an old man's beard was glazed by winter's frost while he waited for a ride across the river. The wait seemed endless. His body became numb and stiff from the frigid north wind.

Selecting a rider

He heard the faint, steady rhythm of approaching hooves galloping along the frozen path. Anxiously, he watched as several horsemen rounded the bend. He let the first one pass by without an effort to get his attention. Then another passed by, and another.

> **LIGHT from the BIBLE**
>
> *"Therefore, as God's chosen people, holy and dearly loved, clothe yourselves with compassion, kindness, humility, gentleness and patience."*
>
> COLOSSIANS 3:12

Finally, the last rider neared the spot where the old man sat like a snow statue. As this one drew near, the old man caught the rider's eye and said, "Sir, would you mind giving an old man a ride to the other side? There doesn't appear to be a passageway by foot."Reining his horse, the rider replied, "Sure thing. Hop aboard."

All the way home

Seeing the old man was unable to lift his half-frozen body from the ground, the horseman dismounted and helped the old man onto the horse. The horseman took the old man not just across the river, but to his destination, which was just a few miles away.

Quotation to ponder

"Be the living expression of God's kindness; kindness in your face, kindness in your eyes, kindness in your smile, kindness in your warm greeting."

MOTHER TERESA OF CALCUTTA

The horseman's question

As they neared the tiny but cozy cottage, the horseman's curiosity caused him to inquire, "Sir, I noticed that you let several other riders pass by without making an effort to secure a ride. Then I came up and you immediately asked me for a ride. I'm curious why, on such a bitter winter night, you would wait and ask the last rider. What if I had refused and left you there?"

Compassionate eyes

The old man lowered himself slowly down from the horse, looked the rider straight in the eyes, and replied, "I've been around these here parts for some time. I reckon I know people pretty good." The old-timer continued, "I looked into the eyes of the other riders and immediately saw there was no concern for my situation. It would have been useless even to ask them for a ride. But when I looked into your eyes, kindness and compassion were evident. I knew, then and there, that your gentle spirit would welcome the opportunity to give me assistance in my time of need."

LIGHT *from the* BIBLE

"Then Peter, filled with the Holy Spirit, said to them: 'Rulers and elders of the people! If we are being called to account today for an act of kindness shown to a cripple and are asked how he was healed, then know this, you and all the people of Israel: It is by the name of Jesus Christ of Nazareth, whom you crucified but whom God raised from the dead, that this man stands before you healed.'"

ACTS 4:8-10

Those heartwarming comments touched the horseman deeply. "I'm most grateful for what you have said," he told the old man. "May I never get too busy in my own affairs that I fail to respond to the needs of others with kindness and compassion."

Hymn to ponder

Kind words toward those you daily meet, Kind words and actions right, Will make this life of ours most sweet, Turn darkness into light.

ISAAC WATTS

Thomas Jefferson
With that, Thomas Jefferson turned his horse around and made his way back to the White House.

Love the living

Sending flowers

A man stopped at a flower shop to order some flowers to be wired to his mother who lived two hundred miles away.

Quotation to ponder

"No man is poor who has had a godly mother."

ABRAHAM LINCOLN

As he got out of his car he noticed a young girl sitting on the curb sobbing. He asked her what was wrong and she replied, "I wanted to buy a red rose for my mother. But I only have seventy-five cents, and a rose costs two dollars."

The man smiled and said, "Come on in with me. I'll buy you a rose." He bought the little girl her rose and ordered his own mother's flowers.

A ride to a cemetery

As they were leaving he offered the girl a ride home. She said, "Yes, please! You can take me to my mother." She directed him to a cemetery, where she placed the rose on a freshly dug grave.

LIGHT *from* the BIBLE

"Honor your father and your mother, as the LORD your God has commanded you."

DEUTERONOMY 5:16

Personal delivery

The man returned to the flower shop, canceled the wire order, picked up a bouquet and drove the two hundred miles to his mother's house.

The prodigal father

Your time and attention

A certain man had two sons and the younger of them said to his father, 'Father, give me the portion of thy time and thy attention, and thy companionship, and thy counsel and thy guidance which falleth to me.'

Paying bills

And the father divided unto him his living, in that he paid his boy's bills and sent him to a select preparatory school and to dancing school and to college and tried to believe that he was doing his complete duty by his son.

Wasted opportunities

And not many days after, the father gathered all his interests and aspirations and ambitions and made a journey into a far country, into a land of stocks and bonds and securities and other things which do not interest a boy, and there he wasted his precious opportunity of being a chum to his son.

And when he had spent the very best of his life and had gained money, but had failed to find any satisfaction, there arose a mighty famine in his heart, and he began to be in want of sympathy and real companionship.

Quotation to ponder

"The family was ordained by God before he established any other institution, even before he established the church."

BILLY GRAHAM

26

LIGHT *from*
the BIBLE

"Jesus continued: 'There was a man who had two sons.
The younger one said to his father, "Father, give me
my share of the estate." So he divided his property
between them. Not long after that, the younger son got
together all he had, set off for a distant country and
there squandered his wealth in wild living. After he
had spent everything, there was a severe famine in
that whole country, and he began to be in need. So he
went and hired himself out to a citizen of that country,
who sent him to his fields to feed pigs. He longed to fill
his stomach with the pods that the pigs were eating,
but no one gave him anything. When he came to his
senses, he said, "How many of my father's hired men
have food to spare, and here I am starving to death!
I will set out and go back to my father and say to him:
Father, I have sinned against heaven and against you.
I am no longer worthy to be called your son; make me
like one of your hired men." So he got up and went to
his father.'"

LUKE 15:11-20

Chairman and president

And the father went and joined himself to one of the clubs of that country and they elected him chairman of the House Committee and President of the club and sent him to the legislature. And he fain would have satisfied himself with the husks that other men did eat, and no man gave him any real friendship.

> **LIGHT from the BIBLE**
>
> *"Fathers, do not embitter your children, or they will become discouraged."*
>
> COLOSSIANS 3:21

He came to himself

But when he came to himself, he said: "How many of my acquaintances have boys whom they understand and who understand them, who talk about their boys and associate with their boys, and seem perfectly happy in the comradeship of their sons and I perish here with heart hunger? I will arise and go unto my son and say unto him: 'Son, I have sinned against heaven and in thy sight and am no more worthy to be called thy father. Make me one of thy acquaintances.'"

> **LIGHT from the BIBLE**
>
> *"Fathers, do not exasperate your children; instead, bring them up in the training and instruction of the Lord."*
>
> EPHESIANS 6:4

The son drew back

But while he was yet afar off his son saw him and was moved with astonishment, and instead of running and falling on his neck, he drew back and was ill at ease. And the father said unto him, "Son, I have sinned against heaven and in thy sight. I have not been a father to you, and I am no more worthy to be called thy father. Forgive me now and let me be your chum."

Too late

But the son said; "Not so, for it is too late. There was a time when I wanted your companionship and advice and counsel, but you were too busy. I got the information and the companionship, but I got the wrong kind, and now, alas, I am wrecked in soul and body. It is too late – too late – too late."

Quotations to ponder

"Children want their parents more than they want the junk we buy them."

JAMES C. DOBSON

"I am not to neglect my family."

D. L. MOODY

"Neglect of children is one of the greatest sins, and it is the highest degree of impiety."

JOHN CHRYSOSTOM

Love and time

Feelings

Once upon a time, there was an island where all the feelings lived: Happiness, Sadness, Knowledge, and all of the others, including Love.

One day it was announced to the feelings that the island would sink, so all constructed boats and left. Except for Love. Love was the only one who stayed. Love wanted to hold out until the last possible moment. When the island had almost sunk, Love decided to ask for help.

Richness

Richness was passing by Love in a grand boat. Love said, "Richness, can you take me with you?"

Richness answered, "No, I can't. There is a lot of gold and silver in my boat. There is no place here for you."

Vanity

Love decided to ask Vanity who was also passing by in a beautiful vessel. "Vanity, please help me!"

"I can't help you, Love. You are all wet and might damage my boat," Vanity answered.

Quotation to ponder

"If you knew the whole Bible, and the sayings of all the philosophers, how would this benefit you unless you had the love and grace of God?"

THOMAS À KEMPIS

LIGHT *from the* BIBLE

"Though I speak with the tongues of men and of angels, and have not charity, I am become as sounding brass, or a tinkling cymbal. Charity suffereth long, and is kind; charity envieth not; charity vaunteth not itself, is not puffed up,
Doth not behave itself unseemly, seeketh not her own, is not easily provoked, thinketh no evil;
Rejoiceth not in iniquity, but rejoiceth in the truth; Beareth all things, believeth all things, hopeth all things, endureth all things."

1 CORINTHIANS 13:1,4-7 KJV

Sadness

Sadness was close by so Love asked, "Sadness, let me go with you."

"Oh . . . Love, I am so sad that I need to be by myself!"

Happiness

Happiness passed by Love, too, but she was so happy that she did not even hear when Love called her.

Who helped me?

Suddenly, there was a voice, "Come, Love, I will take you." It was an elder. So blessed and overjoyed, Love even forgot to ask the elder where they were going. When they arrived at dry land, the elder went her own way. Realizing how much was owed the elder, Love asked Knowledge, another elder, "Who Helped me?"

"It was Time," Knowledge answered.

"Time?" asked Love. "But why did Time help me?" Knowledge smiled with deep wisdom and answered, "Because only Time is capable of understanding how valuable Love is."

31

Wealth, success, love

Three old men

A woman came out of her house and saw three old men with long white beards sitting in her front yard. She did not recognize them. She said, "I don't think I know you, but you must be hungry. Please come in and have something to eat."

"Is the man of the house home?" they asked.

"No," she said. "He's out."

"Then we cannot come in," they replied.

In the evening when her husband came home, she told him what had happened. "Go tell them I am home and invite them in," he said to his wife.

The woman went out and invited the men in.

"We don't go into a house together," they replied.

"Why is that?" she wanted to know.

One of the old men explained: "His name is Wealth," he said, pointing to one of his friends. "He is Success," he said pointing to the other, "and I am Love." Then he added, "Now go in and discuss with your husband which one of us you want in your home."

> **LIGHT from the BIBLE**
>
> *"And now abideth faith, hope, charity, these three; but the greatest of these is charity."*
>
> 1 CORINTHIANS 13:13 KJV

Wealth, Success, or Love?

The woman went in and told her husband what

was said. Her husband was overjoyed.

"How nice," he said. "Since that is the case, let us invite Wealth. Let him come and fill our home with wealth."

His wife disagreed. "My dear, why don't we invite Success?"

Their daughter-in-law was listening from the corner of the room. She jumped in with her own suggestion: "Would it not be better to invite Love. Our home will be filled with love."

Quotation to ponder

"Charity should begin at himself."

JOHN WYCLIFFE

"Let us heed our daughter-in-law's advice," said the husband to his wife. "Go out and invite Love to be our guest."

Love invited in

The woman went out and asked the three old men, "Which one of you is Love? Please come in and be our guest."

Love got up and started walking toward the house. The other two also got up and followed him.

Surprised, the lady asked Wealth and Success: "I only invited Love, why are you coming in?"

The old men replied together: "If you had invited Wealth or Success the other two of us would've stayed out, but since you invited Love, wherever he goes we go with him."

Wherever there is Love there is also Wealth and Success!

Perseverance

John Roebling

*I*n 1883, a creative engineer named John Roebling was
inspired by the idea of building a spectacular bridge
connecting New York with the Long Island.
However, bridge building experts throughout the world
thought that this was an impossible feat. They told Roebling
to forget the idea. It just could not be done. It was not
practical. It had never been done before.

**LIGHT *from*
the BIBLE**

*"You need to
persevere."*

HEBREWS 10:36

His vision

Roebling could not ignore the
vision he had in his mind of
this bridge. He thought about it
all the time and he knew deep
in his heart that it could be
done. He just had to share the dream with someone
else. After much discussion and persuasion he managed
to convince his son Washington, an up-and-coming
engineer, that the bridge in fact could be built.

Father and son partnership

Working together for the first time, the father and son
developed concepts of how it could be accomplished
and how the obstacles could be overcome. With great
excitement and inspiration, and the headiness of a wild
challenge before them, they hired their crew and began
to build their dream bridge.

Brain damage

The project started well, but when it was only a few months underway a tragic accident on the site took the life of John Roebling. Washington was injured and left brain damaged. He could not walk or talk or even move.

Everyone had a negative comment to make and felt that the project should be scrapped since the Roeblings were the only ones who knew how the bridge could be built. In spite of his handicap Washington was never discouraged and still had a burning desire to complete the bridge and his mind was still as sharp as ever.

Quotation to ponder

"Our motto must continue to be perseverance. And ultimately I trust the Almighty will crown our efforts with success."

WILLIAM WILBERFORCE

Washington's hospital bed

He tried to inspire and pass on his enthusiasm to some of his friends, but they were too daunted by the task. As he lay on his bed in his hospital room, with the sunlight streaming through the windows, a gentle breeze blew the flimsy white curtains apart and he was able to see the sky and the tops of the trees outside for just a moment.

Moving one finger

It seemed that there was a message for him not to give up. Suddenly an idea hit him. All he could do was move one finger and he decided to make the best use of it. By moving this, he slowly developed a code of communication with his wife.

Underway again

He touched his wife's arm with that finger, indicating to her that he wanted her to call the engineers again. Then he used the same method of tapping her arm to tell the engineers what to do. It seemed foolish but the project was under way again.

Thirteen long years

For thirteen years Washington tapped out his instructions with his finger on his wife's arm, until the bridge was finally completed.

The Brooklyn Bridge

Today the spectacular Brooklyn Bridge stands in all its glory as a tribute to the triumph of one man's indomitable spirit and his determination not to be defeated by circumstances. It is also a tribute to the

engineers and their team work, and to their faith in a man who was considered mad by half the world. It stands too as a tangible monument to the love and devotion of his wife who for thirteen long years patiently decoded the messages of her husband and told the engineers what to do.

Quotation to ponder

"Who am I? When I was 7 years old my family was forced out of their home on a legal technicality, and I had to work to help support them.

At age 9 my mother died.

At 22, I lost my job as a store clerk. I wanted to go to law school, but my education wasn't good enough.

At 23, I went into debt to become a partner in a small store.

At 26, my business partner died, leaving me a huge debt that took years to repay.

At 28, after courting a girl for four years I asked her to marry me. She said no.

At 37, on my third try, I was elected to the US Congress, but two years later I failed to be re-elected.

At 41, my four-year-old son died.

At 45, I ran for the Senate and lost.

At 47, I failed as the vice-presidential candidate.

At 51, I was elected president of the United States. Who am I? My name was Abraham Lincoln."

ABRAHAM LINCOLN

Back from Vietnam

A favor declined

A soldier was finally coming home after fighting in Vietnam. He called his parents from San Francisco.

"Mom and Dad, I'm coming home, but I've a favor to ask. I have a friend I'd like to bring home with me."

"Sure," they replied, "we'd love to meet him."

"There's something you should know," the son continued, "he was badly injured in the fighting. He stepped on a land mind and lost an arm and a leg. He has nowhere else to go, and I want him to come live with us."

"I'm sorry to hear that, son. Maybe we can help him find somewhere to live."

LIGHT from the BIBLE

"(Jonathan . . . had a son who was lame in both feet . . . His name was Mephibosheth.) . . . David asked, 'Is there anyone still left of the house of Saul to whom I can show kindness for Jonathan's sake?' . . . When Mephibosheth son of Jonathan, the son of Saul, came to David, he bowed down to pay him honor. David said, 'Mephibosheth!' 'Your servant,' he replied. 'Don't be afraid,' David said to him, 'for I will surely show you kindness for the sake of your father Jonathan. I will restore to you all the land that belonged to your grandfather Saul, and you will always eat at my table.'"

2 SAMUEL 4:4; 9:1, 6-7

"No, Mom and Dad, I want him to live with us."

"Son," said the father, "you don't know what you're asking. Someone with such a handicap would be a terrible burden on us. We have our own lives to live, and we can't let something like this interfere with our lives. I think you should just come home and forget about this guy. He'll find a way to live on his own."

No more contact

The son hung up the phone. The parents heard nothing more from him. A few days later, however, they received a call from the San Francisco police. Their son had died after falling from a building, they were told. The police believed it was suicide. The grief-stricken parents flew to San Francisco and were taken to the city morgue to identify the body of their son. They recognized him, but to their horror they also discovered something they didn't know, their son had only one arm and one leg.

Quotation to ponder

"One's attitude toward a handicap determines its impact on his life."

JAMES C. DOBSON

Puppies for sale

A little boy

A farmer had some puppies he needed to sell. He painted a sign advertising the pups and set about nailing it to a post on the edge of his yard. As he was driving the last nail into the post, he felt a tug on his overalls. He looked down into the eyes of a little boy.

> **LIGHT** *from* *the* **BIBLE**
>
> *"Rejoice with those who rejoice; mourn with those who mourn. Live in harmony with one another. Do not be proud, but be willing to associate with people of low position.*
> *Do not be conceited."*
>
> ROMANS 12:15-16

"Mister," he said, "I want to buy one of your puppies."

"Well," said the farmer, as he rubbed the sweat off the back of his neck, "these puppies come from fine parents and cost a good deal of money."

Thirty-nine cents for a look

The boy dropped his head for a moment. Then reaching deep into his pocket, he pulled out a handful of change and held it up to the farmer. "I've got thirty-nine cents. Is that enough to take a look?"

"Sure," said the farmer.

And with that he let out a whistle, "Here, Dolly!" he called.

Out from the doghouse and down the ramp ran

Dolly followed by four little balls of fur. The little boy pressed his face against the chain link fence. His eyes danced with delight.

The hobbling pup

As the dogs made their way to the fence, the little boy noticed something else stirring inside the doghouse. Slowly another little ball appeared; this one noticeably smaller. Down the ramp it slid. Then in a somewhat awkward manner the little pup began hobbling toward the others, doing its best to catch up....

> ## Quotation to ponder
>
> *"Remember that nothing is small in the eyes of God. Do all that you do with love."*
>
> TERESA OF AVILA

"I want that one," the little boy said, pointing to the runt.

The farmer knelt down at the boy's side and said, "Son, you don't want that puppy. He will never be able to run and play with you like these other dogs would."

The boy's revelation

With that the little boy stepped back from the fence, reached down, and began rolling up one leg of his trousers. In doing so he revealed a steel brace running down both sides of his leg attaching itself to a specially made shoe. Looking back up at the farmer, he said, "You see sir, I don't run too well myself, and he will need someone who understands."

The praying hands

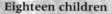

The most often reproduced and widely known work of the German artist Albrecht Dürer, 1471–1528, is the gray and white brush drawing on blue-grounded paper, entitled the "Hands of the Apostle," generally known as "The Praying Hands."

Eighteen children

Back in the fifteenth century, in a tiny village near Nuremberg, lived a family with eighteen children. Just to keep food on the table for this mob, the father and head of the household, a goldsmith by profession, worked almost eighteen hours a day at his trade and any other paying chore he could find in the neighborhood.

Two boys who had a dream

Despite their seemingly hopeless condition, two of Albrecht Dürer's elder children had a dream. They both wanted to pursue their talent for art, but they knew full well that their father would never be financially able to send either of them to Nuremberg to study at the Academy.

> **LIGHT** *from the* **BIBLE**
>
> *"Be devoted to one another in brotherly love. Honor one another above yourselves."*
>
> ROMANS 12:10

Quotation to ponder

"Brotherly love is still the distinguishing badge of every true Christian."

MATTHEW HENRY

Brotherly love

After many long discussions at night in their crowded bed, the two boys finally worked out a pact. They would toss a coin. The loser would go down into the nearby mines and, with his earnings, support his brother while he attended the academy.

Then, when that brother who won the toss completed his studies, in four years, he would support the other brother at the academy, either with sales of his artwork or, if necessary, also by laboring in the mines. They tossed a coin on a Sunday morning after church. Albrecht Dürer won the toss and went off to Nuremberg.

Albert and Albrecht

Albert went down into the dangerous mines and, for the next four years, financed his brother, whose work at the academy was almost an immediate sensation. Albrecht's etchings, his woodcuts, and his oils were far better than those of most of his professors, and by the time he graduated, he was beginning to earn considerable fees for his commissioned works.

Years of sacrifice

When the young artist returned to his village, the Dürer family held a festive dinner on their lawn to celebrate Albrecht's

LIGHT *from the* **BIBLE**

"Love one another."

JOHN 13:34

triumphant homecoming. After a long and memorable meal, punctuated with music and laughter, Albrecht rose from his honored position at the head of the table to drink a toast to his beloved brother for the years of sacrifice that had enabled Albrecht to fulfill his ambition.

"Albert, blessed brother"

His closing words were, "And now, Albert, blessed brother of mine, now it is your turn. Now you can go to Nuremberg to pursue your dream, and I will take care of you."

All heads turned in eager expectation to the far end of the table where Albert sat, tears streaming down his pale face, shaking his lowered head from side to side while he sobbed and repeated, over and over, "No, no, no, no."

"Look at my hands"

Finally, Albert rose and wiped the tears from his cheeks. He glanced down the long table at the faces he loved, and then, holding his hands close to his right cheek, he said softly, "No, brother. I cannot go to Nuremberg. It is too late for me. Look, look what four years in the mines have done to my hands! The bones in every finger have been smashed at least once, and lately I have been suffering from arthritis so badly in my right hand that I cannot even hold a glass to return your toast, much less make delicate lines on parchment or canvas with a pen or a brush. No, brother, for me it is too late."

Albrecht's success

Today, Albrecht Dürer's hundreds of masterful portraits, pen and silver-point sketches, watercolors, charcoals, woodcuts, and copper engravings hang in every great museum in the world. But most people are familiar with only one of Albrecht Dürer's works. A reproduction of it hangs in countless homes and offices.

Homage to Albert

One day, to pay homage to Albert for all that he had sacrificed, Albrecht Dürer painstakingly drew his brother's abused hands with palms together and thin fingers stretched skyward. He called his powerful drawing simply "Hands," but the entire world almost immediately opened their hearts to his great masterpiece and renamed his tribute of love "The Praying Hands."

Quotation to ponder

"We cannot be truly Christian people so long as we flaunt the central teachings of Jesus: brotherly love and the Golden Rule."

MARTIN LUTHER KING, JR.

Colors of the rainbow

A quarrel

Once upon a time the colors of the world started to quarrel: all claimed that they were the best, the most important, the most useful, the favorite.

LIGHT *from the* **BIBLE**

"But in fact God has arranged the parts in the body, every one of them, just as he wanted them to be. If they were all one part, where would the body be? As it is, there are many parts, but one body."

1 CORINTHIANS 12:18-20

Green

Green said: "Clearly I am the most important. I am the sign of life and of hope. I was chosen for grass, trees, leaves – without me, all animals would die. Look over the countryside and you will see that I am in the majority."

Blue

Blue interrupted: "You only think about the earth, but consider the sky and the sea. It is the water that is the basis of life and drawn up by the clouds from the deep sea. The sky gives space and peace and serenity. Without my peace, you would all be nothing."

Yellow

Yellow chuckled: "You are all so serious. I bring laughter, gaiety, and warmth into the world. The sun is yellow, the moon is yellow, the stars are yellow. Every time you look at a sunflower, the whole world starts to smile. Without me there would be no fun."

Orange

Orange started to blow her trumpet: "I am the color of health and strength. I may be scarce, but I am precious for I serve the needs of human life. I carry the most important vitamins. Think of carrots, pumpkins, oranges, mangoes, and paw paws. I don't hang around all the time, but when I fill the sky at sunrise or sunset, my beauty is so striking that no one gives another thought to any of you."

Red

Red could stand it no longer. He shouted out: "I am the ruler of all of you. I am blood – life's blood! I am the color of danger and of bravery. I am willing to fight for a cause. I bring fire into the blood. Without me, the earth would be as empty as the moon. I am the color of passion and of love, the red rose, the poinsettia and the poppy."

Purple

Purple rose up to his full height. He was very tall and spoke with great pomp: "I am the color of royalty and

LIGHT *from the* BIBLE

*"The eye cannot say to the hand, 'I don't need you!'
And the head cannot say to the feet, 'I don't need you!'
On the contrary, those parts of the body that seem to be
weaker are indispensable, and the parts that we think
are less honorable we treat with special honor. And the
parts that are unpresentable are treated with special
modesty, while our presentable parts need no special
treatment. But God has combined the members of the
body and has given greater honor to the parts that
lacked it, so that there should be no division in the
body, but that its parts should have equal concern for
each other. If one part suffers, every part suffers with
it; if one part is honored, every part rejoices with it."*

1 CORINTHIANS 12:21-26

power. Kings, chiefs, and bishops have always chosen
me for I am the sign of authority and wisdom. People
do not question me – they listen and obey."

Indigo
Finally, indigo spoke, much more quietly than all the
others. "You hardly notice me, but without me you all
become superficial. I represent thought and reflection,
twilight and deep water. You need me for balance and
contrast, for prayer and inner peace."

A thunderstorm
And so the colors went on boasting, each convinced of
his or her own superiority. Their quarreling became

louder and louder. Suddenly there was a startling flash of bright lightening and thunder rolled and boomed.

Rain started to pour down relentlessly. The colors crouched down in fear, drawing close to one another for comfort. In the midst of the clamor, rain began to speak: "You foolish colors, fighting amongst yourselves, each trying to dominate the rest. Don't you know that you were each made for a special purpose, unique and different? Join hands with one another and come to me."

Joined hands

Doing as they were told, the colors united and joined hands. The rain continued: "From now on, when it rains, each of you will stretch across the sky in a great bow of color as a reminder that you can all live in peace."

> ### Quotation to ponder
>
> *"Matters non-essential should not be the basis of argument among Christians."*
>
> JOHN CALVIN

The Elephant Man

The movie The Elephant Man tells the true story of John Merrick. Merrick was born in the slums of England in 1862, and almost from birth experienced massive rejection due to his grotesque appearance. Merrick suffered abnormalities that resulted in a large and severely misshapen head, loose, rough skin, and twisted arms and legs.

Rejected

His mother loved him dearly, but died when he was ten. His new stepmother didn't take to him, and at twelve, he was expected to work to contribute to the family finances. After two years working in a cigar shop he was dismissed because his deformities meant he could not keep up the required pace. His father found him a job, of all things, as a door-to-door salesman. This only accentuated Merrick's self-loathing. When people opened their doors and saw him people would literally scream and slam the door in his face. Those who knew who he was, refused to answer their doors. After this "failure" Merrick's father began beating him. Merrick wound up on the street and was rescued by a kindly uncle, the only person who would help him

> **LIGHT** *from the* **BIBLE**
>
> *". . . according to his compassion and many kindnesses."*
>
> ISAIAH 63:7

out. Not wishing to further burden his uncle, Merrick left to live in a squalid workhouse for drunks, cripples, and the retarded.

Observed like a caged animal
His life there was soon so miserable that he offered himself to a carnival owner as a sideshow act. Merrick was a hit. People would pay money to line up and observe him like some animal in a zoo. But the carnival finally provided him with security and a place he belonged. It was while the sideshow was in London that Merrick met Dr. Frederick Treves. Disgusted by Merrick's treatment, Treves wanted to help. He gave Merrick his card, but lost track of him. The police started clamping down on the sideshows, so Merrick was sent to Belgium to work in a sideshow there. But when Belgian police also clamped down Merrick was forced to make his way back to England. But as he limped down Liverpool Street station, foul smelling and misshapen, a crowd gathered simply to watch him. The police took him aside to sort things out, but Merrick's speech was so slurred by his deformities that they couldn't understand him. It was at this point Merrick showed them Dr. Treves' card.

Quotation to ponder

"He who plants kindness gathers love."

ST. BASIL

Dr. Treves

The police sent for Dr. Treves and Treves rushed to assist
Merrick. He took Merrick back to a London hospital and
began a newspaper appeal for funds to help Merrick.
The response was very warm, and soon enough was
collected so that Merrick could live in his own house in
the hospital grounds with permission to live there
permanently.

Transformation

Treves' care marked a real turning point for Merrick.
At first Merrick would act like a frightened child and
hide when anyone came into his room, but over time
he began to speak to some people. Dr. Treves discovered
that Merrick was in fact highly intelligent and sought to
nurture his growth.

Acceptance by women

Yet Merrick's greatest hurdle was still to fall. All his life
Merrick had known only fear and rejection from
women. They had literally run from him. So Dr. Treves
asked an attractive widow he knew if she could come
into Merrick's room, smile at him, and shake his hand.
When she did Merrick broke down into a ball of tears,
later telling Treves that she was the first woman in his
life apart from his mother to have showed him kindness.

New friends

That was a breakthrough moment for Merrick. In the
coming years more and more people, women included,

LIGHT *from the* BIBLE
". . . be compassionate . . ."
1 PETER 3:8

would meet him and show him kindness. He began
meeting countesses and duchesses. He even had many
visits and letters from the Princess of Wales, forming a
friendship with her. Throughout this time Dr. Treves
reports Merrick changed dramatically. He began to
develop some self-confidence, to spend time traveling in
the country, to discuss poetry with another new friend,
Sir Walter Steel.

Liberated

Merrick died in April 1890. His deformities had never
allowed him to sleep lying down as most people do.
He had to sleep in a sitting position, his head resting on
his knees. He apparently tried one night to sleep lying
down, to be more "normal," and sadly dislocated his
neck and died.

Merrick's life was made tragic not by his deformities but
by the response people made
to them. Merrick's story shows
the power of love and
acceptance. Rejected all his life,
treated as a "thing," it was the
loving welcome of others that
liberated him to become all he
could be.

Quotation to ponder

*"If you want to be
holy, be kind."*
FREDERICK BUECHNER

Forgiven forever

Lisa's show box

L isa sat on the floor of her old room, staring at the box that lay in front of her. It was an old shoebox that she had decorated to become a memory box many years before. Stickers and penciled flowers covered the top and sides. Its edges were worn, the corners of the lid taped so as to keep their shape.

It had been three years since Lisa last opened the box. A sudden move to Boston had kept her from packing it. But now that she was back home, she took the time to look again at the memories.

Fingering the corners of the box and stroking its cover, Lisa pictured in her mind what was inside.

There was a photo of the family trip to the Grand Canyon, a note from her friend telling her that Nick Bicotti liked her, and the Indian arrowhead she had found while on her senior class trip.

The painful memory

One by one, she remembered the items in the box, lingering over the

> **LIGHT *from the* BIBLE**
>
> *"Out of the depths I cry to you, O LORD;*
> *O Lord, hear my voice.*
> *Let your ears be attentive to my cry for mercy.*
> *If you, O LORD, kept a record of sins,*
> *O Lord, who could stand?*
> *But with you there is forgiveness;*
> *therefore you are feared."*
>
> PSALM 130:1-4

sweetest, until she came to the last and only painful memory. She knew what it looked like – a single sheet of paper upon which lines had been drawn to form boxes, four hundred and ninety of them to be exact. And each box contained a check mark, one for each time.

Quotation to ponder

"Even the most advanced believer has need, as long as he continues in the flesh, to pray daily for the forgiveness of sins."

CHARLES HODGE

The story behind the boxes

"How many times must I forgive my brother?" the disciple Peter had asked Jesus. "Seven times?" Lisa's Sunday school teacher had read Jesus' surprise answer to the class. "Seventy times seven."

Lisa had leaned over to her brother Brent as the teacher continued reading. "How many times is that?" she whispered.

Brent, though two years younger, was smarter than she was. "Four hundred and ninety," Brent wrote on the corner of his Sunday school paper. Lisa saw the message, nodded, and sat back in her chair. She watched her brother as the lesson continued.

Brent

He was small for his age, with narrow shoulders and short arms. His glasses were too large for his face, and his hair always matted in swirls. He bordered on being a nerd, but his incredible skills at everything, especially music, made him popular with his classmates.

Brent had learned to play the piano at age four, the clarinet at age seven, and had just begun to play oboe. His music teachers said he'd be a famous musician someday. There was only one thing at which Lisa was better than Brent – basketball. They played it almost every afternoon after school.

Brent could have refused to play, but he knew that it was Lisa's only joy in the midst of her struggles to get Cs and Ds at school.

> **LIGHT** *from the* **BIBLE**
>
> *". . . in him we have redemption . . . the forgiveness of sins."*
>
> EPHESIANS 1:7

Basketball

Lisa's attention came back to her Sunday school teacher as the woman finished the lesson and closed with prayer. That same Sunday afternoon found brother and sister playing basketball in the driveway. It was then that the counting had begun. Brent was guarding Lisa as she dribbled toward the basket. He had tried to bat the ball away, got his face near her elbow, and took a shot on the chin. "Ow!", he cried out and turned away.

Lisa saw her opening and drove to the basket. She gloated over her success but stopped when she saw Brent. "You okay?" she asked. Brent shrugged his shoulders.

"Sorry," Lisa said. "Really. It was a cheap shot."

"It's all right. I forgive you," he said. A thin smile

then formed on his face. "Just 489 more times though."

"What do you mean?" Lisa asked.

"You know. What we learned in Sunday school today. You're supposed to forgive someone 490 times. I just forgave you, so now you have 489 left," he kidded. The two of them laughed at the thought of keeping track of every time Lisa had done something to Brent. They were sure she had gone past 490 long ago.

Battleship

The rain interrupted their game, and the two moved indoors. "Wanna play Battleship?" Lisa asked. Brent agreed, and they were soon on the floor of the living room with their game boards in front of them. Each took turns calling out a letter and number combination, hoping to hit each other's ships.

Lisa knew she was in trouble as the game went on. Brent had only lost one ship out of five. Lisa had lost three. Desperate to win, she found herself leaning over the edge of Brent's barrier ever so slightly. She was thus able to see where Brent had placed two of his ships. She quickly evened the score.

Quotation to ponder

"Community is not possible without the willingness to forgive one another 'seventy-seven times.' Forgiveness is the cement of community life. Forgiveness holds us together through good times and bad times, and it allows us to grow in mutual love."

HENRY J. NOUWEN

Pleased, Lisa searched once more for the location of the last two ships. She peered over the barrier again, but this time Brent caught her in the act. "Hey, you're cheating!" He stared at her in disbelief.

Lisa's face turned red. Her lips quivered. "I'm sorry," she said, staring at the carpet. There was not much Brent could say. He knew Lisa sometimes did things like this. He felt sorry that Lisa found so few things she could do well. It was wrong for her to cheat, but he knew the temptation was hard for her.

"Okay, I forgive you," Brent said. Then he added with a small laugh, "I guess it's down to 488 now, huh?"

A forgiving spirit

"Yeah, I guess so." She returned his kindness with a weak smile and added, "Thanks for being my brother, Brent."

Brent's forgiving spirit gripped Lisa, and she wanted him to know how sorry she was. It was that evening that she had made the chart with the 490 boxes. She showed it to him before he went to bed.

"We can keep track of every time I mess up and you forgive me," she said. "See, I'll put a check in each box – like this." She placed two marks in the upper left-hand boxes.

"These are for today." Brent raised his hands to protest. "You don't need to keep a record."

"Yes I do!" Lisa interrupted. "You're always forgiving me, and I want to keep track. Just let me do this!" She

LIGHT *from the* BIBLE

"Then Peter came to Jesus and asked, 'Lord, how many times shall I forgive my brother when he sins against me? Up to seven times?' Jesus answered, 'I tell you, not seven times, but seventy-seven times.'"

MATTHEW 18:21-22

went back to her room and tacked the chart to her bulletin board.

There were many opportunities to fill in the chart in the years that followed. She once told the kids at school that Brent talked in his sleep and called out Rhonda Hill's name, even though it wasn't true. The teasing caused Brent days and days of misery. When she realized how cruel she had been, Lisa apologized sincerely. That night she marked box number ninety-six.

Two hundred and eleven

Forgiveness number two hundred and eleven came in the tenth grade when Lisa failed to bring home his English book. Brent had stayed home sick that day and had asked her to bring it so he could study for a quiz. She forgot and he got a C.

Quotation to ponder

"It is in pardoning that we are pardoned."

FRANCIS OF ASSISI

> ### LIGHT *from the* BIBLE
>
> *"The punishment inflicted on him by the majority is sufficient for him. Now instead, you ought to forgive and comfort him, so that he will not be overwhelmed by excessive sorrow. I urge you, therefore, to reaffirm your love for him."*
>
> 2 CORINTHIANS 2:6-8

Number three hundred and ninety-three was for lost keys. Number four hundred and eighteen was for the extra bleach she put in the washer, which ruined his favorite polo shirt. Number four hundred and forty-nine was for the dent she had put in his car when she had borrowed it.

Four hundred and ninety

There was a small ceremony when Lisa checked number four hundred and ninety. She used a gold pen for the check mark, had Brent sign the chart, and then placed it in her memory box.

"I guess that's the end," Lisa said. "No more screw-ups from me anymore!"

Brent just laughed. "Yeah, right."

Four hundred and ninety-one

Number four hundred and ninety-one was just another one of Lisa's careless mistakes, but its hurt lasted a lifetime. Brent had become all that his music teachers said he would. Few could play the oboe better than he. In his fourth year at the best music school in the United States, he received the opportunity of a lifetime – a chance to try out for New York City's great orchestra.

The tryout would be held sometime during the following two weeks. It would be the fulfillment of his young dreams. But he never got the chance.

"Two-thirty on the tenth"

Brent had been out when the call about the tryout came to the house. Lisa was the only one home and on her way out the door, eager to get to work on time.

"Two-thirty on the tenth," the secretary said on the phone. Lisa did not have a pen, but she told herself that she could remember it.

"Got it. Thanks." I can remember that, she thought. But she did not. It was a week later around the dinner table that Lisa realized her mistake.

"So, Brent," his mom asked him, "When do you try out?"

"Don't know yet. They're supposed to call." Lisa froze in her seat.

"Oh, no!" she blurted out loud. "What's today's date? Quick!"

"It's the twelfth," her dad answered. "Why?" A terrible pain ripped through Lisa's heart. She buried her face in her hands, crying. "Lisa, what's the matter?" her mother asked.

Quotation to ponder

"It is idle for us to say that we know that God has forgiven us if we are not loving and forgiving ourselves."

D. MARTYN LLOYD-JONES

Through sobs Lisa explained what had happened. "It was two days ago, the tryout, two-thirty, the call came, last week."

Brent sat back in his chair, not believing Lisa.

No joke

"Is this one of your jokes, sis?" he asked, though he could tell her misery was real. She shook her head, still unable to look at him.

"Then I really missed it?" She nodded.

Brent ran out of the kitchen without a word. He did not come out of his room the rest of the evening. Lisa tried once to knock on the door, but she could not face him. She went to her room where she cried bitterly.

Suddenly she knew what she had to do. She had ruined Brent's life. He could never forgive her for that. She had failed her family, and there was nothing to do but to leave home. Lisa packed her pickup truck in the middle of the night and left a note behind, telling her folks she'd be all right. She began writing a note to Brent, but her words sounded empty to her. Nothing I say could make a difference anyway, she thought.

LIGHT *from the* BIBLE

"Therefore, I tell you, her many sins have been forgiven – for she loved much. But he who has been forgiven little loves little."

LUKE 7:47

Waitress in Boston

Two days later she got a job as a waitress in Boston. She found an apartment not too far from the restaurant. Her parents tried many times to reach her, but Lisa ignored their letters.

Quotation to ponder

"Forgiving is one of the most unbelievable, one of the most indispensable Gospel realities for anyone who wants to follow Christ."

BROTHER ROGER OF TAIZÉ

"It's too late," she wrote them once. "I've ruined Brent's life, and I'm not coming back."

Lisa did not think she would ever see home again. But one day in the restaurant where she worked she saw a face she knew. "Lisa!" said Mrs. Nelson, looking up from her plate. "What a surprise."

The woman was a friend of Lisa's family from back home. "I was so sorry to hear about your brother," Mrs. Nelson said softly. "Such a terrible accident. But we can be thankful that he died quickly. He didn't suffer."

Lisa stared at the woman in shock.

"Wh-hat," she finally stammered.

It couldn't be! Her brother? Dead? The woman quickly saw that Lisa did not know about the accident. She told the girl the sad story of the speeding car, the rush to the hospital, the doctors working over Brent. But all they could do was not enough to save him.

Lisa's return

Lisa returned home that afternoon. Now she found herself in her room thinking about her brother as she held the small box that held some of her memories of him. Sadly, she opened the box and peered inside. It was as she remembered, except for one item – Brent's

LIGHT *from the* BIBLE

"For if you forgive men when they sin against you,
your heavenly Father will also forgive you."

MATTHEW 6:14

chart. It was not there. In its place, at the bottom of the box, was an envelope. Her hands shook as she tore it open and removed a letter.

The first page read:

> Dear Lisa,
> It was you who kept count,
> not me. But if you're
> stubborn enough to keep
> count, use the new chart
> I've made for you.
> Love, Brent

Lisa turned to the second page where she found a chart just like the one she had made as a child, but on this one the lines were drawn in perfect precision. And unlike the chart she had kept, there was but one check mark in the upper left-hand corner. Written in red felt tip pen over the entire page were the words:

"Number 491. Forgiven, forever."

Quotation to ponder

"The offender never pardons."

GEORGE HERBERT

The secret of happiness

An empty life

A beautiful, expensively dressed lady complained to her psychiatrist that she felt that her whole life was empty; it had no meaning.

So the counselor called over the old lady who cleaned the office floors, and then said to the rich lady, "I'm going to ask Mary here to tell you how she found happiness. All I want you to do is listen."

Mary told her story

So the old lady put down her broom and sat on a chair and told her story.

"Well, my husband died of malaria and three months later my only son was killed by a car. I had nobody. I had nothing left. I couldn't sleep; I couldn't eat; I never smiled at anyone, I even thought of taking my own life.

"Then one evening a little kitten followed me home from work. Somehow I felt sorry for that kitten. It was

---

LIGHT *from the* BIBLE

"In everything I did, I showed you that by this kind of hard work we must help the weak, remembering the words the Lord Jesus himself said: 'It is more blessed to give than to receive.'"

ACTS 20:35

---

cold outside, so I decided to let the kitten in. I got it some milk, and it licked the plate clean. Then it purred and rubbed against my leg, and for the first time in months, I smiled. Then I stopped to think; if helping a little kitten could make me smile, maybe doing something for people could make me happy. So the next day I baked some biscuits and took them to a neighbor who was sick in bed. Every day I tried to do something nice for someone. It made me so happy to see them happy. Today, I don't know of anybody who sleeps and eats better than I do. I've found happiness, by giving it to others."

Quotation to ponder

"We deem it a sacred responsibility and genuine opportunity to be faithful stewards of all God has entrusted to us: our time, our talents, and our financial resources. We view all of life as a sacred trust to be used wisely."

MORAVIAN COVENANT
FOR CHRISTIAN LIVING

Tears

When she heard that, the rich lady cried. She had everything that money could buy, but she had lost the things which money cannot buy.

LIGHT *from the* BIBLE

*"When the Son of Man comes in his glory, and all the
angels with him, he will sit on his throne in heavenly
glory. All the nations will be gathered before him, and
he will separate the people one from another as a
shepherd separates the sheep from the goats. He will
put the sheep on his right and the goats on his left.
Then the King will say to those on his right, 'Come,
you who are blessed by my Father; take your
inheritance, the kingdom prepared for you since the
creation of the world. For I was hungry and you gave
me something to eat, I was thirsty and you gave me
something to drink, I was a stranger and you invited
me in, I needed clothes and you clothed me, I was sick
and you looked after me, I was in prison and you came
to visit me.' Then the righteous will answer him, 'Lord,
when did we see you hungry and feed you, or thirsty
and give you something to drink? When did we see you
a stranger and invite you in, or needing clothes and
clothe you? When did we see you sick or in prison and
go to visit you?' The King will reply, 'I tell you the
truth, whatever you did for one of the least of these
brothers of mine, you did for me.'"*

MATTHEW 25:31-40

Heaven and hell

Hell

A man spoke with the Lord about Heaven and Hell. "I will show you Hell," said the Lord. And they went into a room which had a large pot of stew in the middle. The smell was delicious and around the pot sat people who were famished and desperate.

All were holding spoons with very long handless which reached to the pot, but because the handles of the spoons were longer than their arms, it was impossible to get the stew into their mouths. Their suffering was terrible.

Heaven

"Now I will show you Heaven," said the Lord, and they went into an identical room. There was a similar pot of stew and the people had the same identical spoons, but they were well nourished, talking and happy.

At first the man did not understand.

"It is simple," said the Lord. "You see, they have learned to feed each other."

Quotation to ponder

"I believe the single most significant decision I can make on a day-to-day basis is my choice of attitude."

CHARLES R. SWINDOLL

Keep your fork

Terminal illness

There was a woman who had been diagnosed with a terminal illness and had been given three months to live.

So as she was getting her things "in order," she contacted her pastor and had him come to her house to discuss certain aspects of her final wishes.

"A fork in my right hand"

She told him which songs she wanted sung at the service, what scriptures she would like read, and what outfit she wanted to be buried in.

The woman also requested to be buried with her favorite Bible.

Everything was in order and the pastor was preparing to leave when

> **LIGHT *from the* BIBLE**
>
> *"And I heard a loud voice from the throne saying, 'Now the dwelling of God is with men, and he will live with them. They will be his people, and God himself will be with them and be their God. He will wipe every tear from their eyes. There will be no more death or mourning or crying or pain, for the old order of things has passed away.' He who was seated on the throne said, 'I am making everything new!' Then he said, 'Write this down, for these words are trustworthy and true.'"*
>
> REVELATION 21:3-5

the woman suddenly remembered something very important to her.

"There's one more thing," she excitedly.

"What's that?" came the pastor's reply.

"This is very important," the woman continued. "I want to be buried with a fork in my right hand."

The pastor stood looking at the woman, not knowing quite what to say. "That surprises you, doesn't it?" the woman asked.

"Well, to be honest, I'm puzzled by the request," said the pastor.

"Keep your fork"

The woman explained.

"In all my years of attending church socials and potluck dinners I always remember that when the dishes were cleared, someone would inevitably lean over and say, 'Keep your fork.'

It was my favorite part because I knew that something better was coming – like velvety chocolate cake or deep-dish apple pie. Something wonderful and of substance!"

Quotation to ponder

"Hearts on earth say in the course of a joyful experience, 'I don't want this ever to end.' But it invariably does. The hearts of those in heaven say, 'I want this to go on forever.' And it will. There is no better news than this."

J. I. PACKER

LIGHT *from the* BIBLE

*"I eagerly expect and hope that I will in no way be
ashamed, but will have sufficient courage so that now
as always Christ will be exalted in my body, whether
by life or by death. For to me, to live is Christ and to
die is gain. If I am to go on living in the body, this will
mean fruitful labor for me. Yet what shall I choose?
I do not know! I am torn between the two: I desire to
depart and be with Christ, which is better by far; but it
is more necessary for you that I remain in the body."*

PHILIPPIANS 1:20-24

"I want them to wonder"

"So I just want people to see me there in that casket
with a fork in my hand and I want them to wonder,
'What's with the fork?'

"Then I want you to tell them: 'Keep your fork, the
best is yet to come.'"

The pastor's eyes welled up with
tears of joy as he hugged the
woman goodbye.

He knew this would be
one of the last times he
would see her before her
death. But he also knew
that the woman had a
better grasp of heaven that
he did. She knew that
something better was coming.

The funeral

At the funeral people were walking by the woman's casket and they saw the pretty dress she was wearing and her favorite Bible and the fork placed in her right hand.

Over and over, the pastor heard the question, "What's with the fork?" And over and over he smiled.

During his message, the pastor told the people of the conversation he had with the woman shortly before she died.

He also told them about the fork and what it symbolized to her.

The pastor told the people how he could not stop thinking about the fork and told them that they probably would not be able to stop thinking about it either.

He was right.

Quotation to ponder

"Jesus himself is preparing all of us who know him for a most distant journey – more distant even that the trip to the moon. The Lord wants us to be where he is throughout eternity."

JAMES B. IRWIN

The window

The only window

Two men, both seriously ill, occupied the same hospital room. One man was allowed to sit up in his bed for an hour each afternoon to help drain the fluid from his lungs. His bed was next to the room's only window.

The other man had to spend all his time flat on his back. The men talked for hours on end. They spoke of their wives and families, their homes, their jobs, their involvement in the military service, and where they had been on vacation. And every afternoon when the man in the bed by the window could sit up, he would pass the time by describing to his roommate all the things he could see outside the window.

View from the window

The man in the other bed began to live for those one-hour periods where his world would be broadened and enlivened

LIGHT from the BIBLE

"But Timothy has just now come to us from you and has brought good news about your faith and love. He has told us that you always have pleasant memories of us and that you long to see us, just as we also long to see you. Therefore, brothers, in all our distress and persecution we were encouraged about you because of your faith. For now we really live, since you are standing firm in the Lord."

1 THESSALONIANS 3:6-8

Quotation to ponder

"We hurt people by being too busy. Too busy to notice their needs. Too busy to drop that note of comfort or encouragement or assurance of love. Too busy to listen when someone needs to talk. Too busy to care."

BILLY GRAHAM

by all the activity and color of the world outside. The window overlooked a park with a lovely lake. Ducks and swans played on the water while children sailed their model boats. Young lovers walked arm in arm amidst flowers of every color of the rainbow. Grand old trees graced the landscape, and a fine view of the city skyline could be seen in the distance.

As the man by the window described all this in exquisite detail, the man on the other side of the room would close his eyes and imagine the picturesque scene. One warm afternoon the man by the window described a parade passing by. Although the other man couldn't hear the band – he could see it in his mind's eye as the man by the window portrayed it with descriptive words.

Enter jealousy

Then unexpectedly, a sinister thought entered his mind: Why should the other man alone experience all the pleasures of seeing everything while he himself never got to see anything? It didn't seem fair.

At first thought the man felt ashamed. But as the days passed and he missed seeing more sights, his envy eroded into resentment and soon turned him sour. He began to brood and he found himself unable to sleep. He should be by that window – that thought, and only that thought now controlled his life.

He let him die

Late one night, as he lay staring at the ceiling, the man by the window began to cough. He was choking on the fluid in his lungs. The other man watched in the dimly lit room as the struggling man by the window groped for the button to call for help.

Listening from across the room he never moved, never pushed his own button, which would have brought the nurse running in. In less than five minutes the coughing and choking stopped, along with that the sound of breathing. Now there was only silence – deathly silence.

LIGHT *from the* BIBLE

"And we urge you, brothers, warn those who are idle, encourage the timid, help the weak, be patient with everyone."

1 THESSALONIANS 5:14

Move to the window

The following morning the day nurse arrived to bring water for their baths. When she found the lifeless body of the man by the window, she was saddened and called the hospital attendants to take it away. As soon as it seemed appropriate, the other man asked if he could be moved next to the window. The nurse was happy to make the switch, and after making sure he was comfortable, she left him alone. Slowly, painfully, he propped himself up on one elbow to take his first look at the world outside. Finally, he would have the joy of seeing it all himself. He strained to slowly turn to look out the window beside the bed.

It faced a blank wall!

The man asked the nurse what could have compelled his deceased roommate who had described such wonderful things outside this window. The nurse responded that the man was blind and could not even see the wall. She said, "Perhaps he just wanted to encourage you."

> ## Quotation to ponder
>
> "Discouraged people don't need critics. They hurt enough already. They need encouragement. They need a refuge. A willing, caring, available someone."
>
> CHARLES R. SWINDOLL

The Fisherman's Fellowship

The call to fish

There was a group called the Fisherman's Fellowship. They were surrounded by streams and lakes full of hungry fish. They met regularly to discuss the call to fish, the abundance of fish, and the thrill of catching fish. They got excited about fishing!

A philosophy of fishing

Someone suggested that they needed a philosophy of fishing, so they carefully defined and redefined fishing, and the purpose of fishing. They developed fishing strategies and tactics. Then they realized that they had been going at it backwards. They had approached fishing from the point of view of the fisherman, and not from the point of

> ### LIGHT *from the* BIBLE
>
> *"As Jesus was walking beside the Sea of Galilee, he saw two brothers, Simon called Peter and his brother Andrew. They were casting a net into the lake, for they were fishermen. 'Come, follow me,' Jesus said, 'and I will make you fishers of men.' At once they left their nets and followed him. Going on from there, he saw two other brothers, James son of Zebedee and his brother John. They were in a boat with their father Zebedee, preparing their nets. Jesus called them, and immediately they left the boat and their father and followed him."*
>
> MATTHEW 4:18-22

view of the fish. How do fish view the world? How does the fisherman appear to the fish? What do fish eat, and when? These are all good things to know. So they began research studies, and attended conferences on fishing. Some traveled to faraway places to study different kinds of fish, with different habits. Some got PhDs in fishology. But no one had yet gone fishing.

A committee

So a committee was formed to send out fisherman. As prospective fishing places outnumbered fisherman, the committee needed to determine priorities. A priority list of fishing places was posted on bulletin boards in all of the fellowship halls. But still, no one was fishing.

> ## Quotation to ponder
>
> *"Many modern methods of evangelism lead either to an inadequate perception of the gospel (seen less clearly it can be rejected more easily) or to an inadequate preparation for Christian discipleship (a gospel that is all invitation and no demand, all choice and no chosenness, is no basis for costly obedience)."*
>
> OS GUINNESS

A survey

A survey was launched, to find out why. Most did not answer the survey, but from those who did, it was discovered that some felt called to study fish, a few, to furnish fishing equipment, and several to go around encouraging the fishermen. What with meetings, conferences, and seminars, they just simply didn't have time to fish.

> **LIGHT** *from the* **BIBLE**
>
> *"Therefore go and make disciples of all nations, baptizing them in the name of the Father and of the Son and of the Holy Spirit, and teaching them to obey everything I have commanded you. And surely I am with you always, to the very end of the age."*
>
> MATTHEW 28:19-20

Jake goes fishing

Now, Jake was a newcomer to the Fisherman's Fellowship. After one stirring meeting of the Fellowship, Jake went fishing. He tried a few things, got the hang of it, and caught a choice fish. At the next meeting, he told his story, and he was honored for his catch, and then scheduled to speak at all the Fellowship chapters and tell how he did it. Now, because of all the speaking invitations and his election to the board of directors of the Fisherman's Fellowship, Jake no longer has time to go fishing.

The fishers were few

But soon he began to feel restless and empty. He longed to feel the tug on the line once again. So he cut the speaking, he resigned from the board, and he said to a friend, "Let's go fishing." They did, just the two of them, and they caught fish. The members of the Fisherman's Fellowship were many, the fish were plentiful, but the fishers were few.

Quotation to ponder

"If you were an outstandingly gifted evangelist with an international reputation, and if, under God, you could win 1,000 persons for Christ every night of every year, how long would it take you to win the whole world for Christ? Answer, ignoring the population explosion, over 10,000 years. But if you are a true disciple for Christ, and if you are able under God to win just one person to Christ each year; and if you could then train that person to win one other person for Christ each year, how long would it take to win the whole world for Christ? Answer, just 32 years!"

D. JAMES KENNEDY

The wise woman's stone

Request granted

A wise woman who was traveling in the mountains found a precious stone in a stream. The next day she met another traveler who was hungry, and the wise woman opened her bag to share her food. The hungry traveler saw the precious stone and asked the woman to give it to him. She did so without hesitation. The traveler left rejoicing in his good fortune. He knew the stone was worth enough to give him security for a lifetime.

Quotation to ponder

"Knowledge comes, but wisdom lingers."

ALFRED TENNYSON

Second request

But, a few days later, he came back to return the stone to the wise woman. "I've been thinking," he said.

"I know how valuable this stone is, but I give it back in the hope that you can give me something even more precious. Give me what you have within you that enabled you to give me this stone." The man had learned that sometimes it is not the wealth we have but what is inside us that others need.

LIGHT *from the* BIBLE

"He went on: 'What comes out of a man is what makes him "unclean." For from within, out of men's hearts, come evil thoughts, sexual immorality, theft, murder, adultery, greed, malice, deceit, lewdness, envy, slander, arrogance and folly.'"

MARK 7:20-22

I sent you a rowboat

The flood

Aflood came and one very devout man scrambled on the roof of his house. A neighbor came by in a rowboat and says, "Come with me!"

The man says, "No, the Lord will save me!"

The police come by in a powerboat and say, "Come with us!"

Again, the man replies, "No, the Lord will save me!" Finally, a helicopter comes by, "Come aboard!" the pilot says.

"No, The Lord will save me!"

Finally, the waters rise and the man drowns.

Quotation to ponder

"Thus I entreat you neither to entrust everything to God and then fall asleep, nor to think, when you are striving diligently, that you will achieve everything by your own efforts."

JOHN CHRYSOSTOM

Complaint rebuffed

When he arrives at the pearly gates, he meets the Lord and asks, "Lord, why didn't you save me?" The Lord replies, "I sent you a rowboat, a powerboat and a helicopter. What more did you want?"

LIGHT *from the* BIBLE

[On board a ship about to be shipwrecked] "Just before dawn Paul urged them all to eat. . . .
'You need it to survive. Not one of you will lose a single hair from his head.' After he said this, he took some bread and gave thanks to God in front of them all. Then he broke it and began to eat."

ACTS 27:33-35

The emperor's seed

Choosing a successor

Once there was an emperor in the Far East who was growing old and knew it was coming time to choose his successor. Instead of choosing one of his assistants or one of his own children, he decided to do something different.

He called all the young people in the kingdom together one day. He said, "It has come time for me to step down and to choose the next emperor. I have decided to choose one of you." The kids were shocked! But the emperor continued. "I am going to give each one of you a seed today. One seed. It is a very special seed. I want you to go home, plant the seed, water it, and come back here one year from today with what you have grown from this one seed. I will then judge the plants that you bring to me, and the one I choose will be the next emperor of the kingdom!"

Quotation to ponder

"Set yourself earnestly to discover what you are made to do, and then give yourself passionately to the doing of it."

MARTIN LUTHER KING, JR.

Ling

There was one boy named Ling who was there that day and he, like the others, received a seed. He went home and excitedly told his mother the whole story. She helped him get a pot and some planting soil, and he

LIGHT *from*
the BIBLE

*"Now a man named Ananias, together with his wife
Sapphira, also sold a piece of property. With his wife's
full knowledge he kept back part of the money for
himself, but brought the rest and put it at the apostles'
feet. Then Peter said, 'Ananias, how is it that Satan
has so filled your heart that you have lied to the Holy
Spirit and have kept for yourself some of the money
you received for the land? Didn't it belong to you
before it was sold? And after it was sold, wasn't the
money at your disposal? What made you think of doing
such a thing? You have not lied to men but to God.'
When Ananias heard this, he fell down and died. And
great fear seized all who heard what had happened.
Then the young men came forward, wrapped up his
body, and carried him out and buried him."*

ACTS 5:1-6

planted the seed and watered it carefully. Every day he would water it and watch to see if it had grown.

No growth

After about three weeks, some of the other youths began to talk about their seeds and the plants that were beginning to grow. Ling kept going home and checking his seed, but nothing ever grew. Three weeks, four weeks, five weeks went by. Still nothing.

By now others were talking about their plants but Ling didn't have a plant, and he felt like a failure. Six months went by, still nothing in Ling's pot. He just knew he had killed his seed. Everyone else had trees and tall plants, but he had nothing. Ling didn't say anything to his friends, however. He just kept waiting for his seed to grow.

Ling's empty pot

A year finally went by and all the youths of the kingdom brought their plants to the emperor for inspection. Ling told his mother that he wasn't going to take an empty pot. But she encouraged him to go, and to take his pot, and to be honest about what happened. Ling felt sick to his stomach, but he knew his mother was right. He took his empty pot to the palace.

When Ling arrived, he was amazed at the variety of plants grown by all the other youths. They were beautiful, in all shapes and sizes. Ling put his empty pot on the floor and many of the other kids laughed at him. A few felt sorry for him and just said, "Hey nice try."

The emperor arrives

When the emperor arrived, he surveyed the room and greeted the young people. Ling just tried to hide in the back. "My, what great plants, trees, and flowers you have grown," said the emperor. "Today, one of you will be appointed the next emperor!"

All of a sudden, the emperor spotted Ling at the back of the room with his empty pot. He ordered his guards to bring him to the

> ## Quotation to ponder
>
> *"One desire has been the ruling passion of my life. It is this: That, God's holy ordinances shall be established again in the home, in the school and in the State."*
>
> ABRAHAM KUYPER

LIGHT *from the* BIBLE

"I tell you, use worldly wealth to gain friends for yourselves, so that when it is gone, you will be welcomed into eternal dwellings. Whoever can be trusted with very little can also be trusted with much, and whoever is dishonest with very little will also be dishonest with much.

So if you have not been trustworthy in handling worldly wealth, who will trust you with true riches?"

LUKE 16:9-11

front. Ling was terrified. "The emperor knows I'm a failure! Maybe he will have me killed!"

When Ling got to the front, the emperor asked his name. "My name is Ling," he replied. All the kids were laughing and making fun of him. The emperor asked everyone to quiet down.

"Behold your new emperor"

The emperor looked at Ling, and then announced to the crowd, "Behold your new emperor! His name is Ling!" Ling couldn't believe it. Ling couldn't even grow his seed. How could he be the new emperor?

The emperor's plan revealed

Then the emperor said, "One year ago today, I gave everyone here a seed. I told you to take the seed, plant it, water it, and bring it back to me today. But I gave you all boiled seeds which would not grow. All of you, except Ling, have brought me trees and plants and flowers. When you found that the seed would not grow, you substituted another seed for the one I gave you. Ling was the only one with the courage and honesty to bring me a pot with my seed in it. Therefore, he is the one who will be the new emperor!"

Quotation to ponder

"They took away what should have been my eyes, (But I remembered Milton's Paradise) They took away what should have been my ears, (Beethoven came and wiped away my tears) They took away what should have been my tongue, (But I had talked with God when I was young) He would not let them take away my soul, Possessing that, I still possess the whole."

HELEN KELLER

A vision of the lost

Millions of people

On one of my recent journeys, as I gazed from the coach window, I was led into a train of thought concerning the condition of the multitudes around me. They were living carelessly in the most open and shameless rebellion against God, without a thought for their eternal welfare. As I looked out of the window, I seemed to see them all, millions of people all around me given up to their drink and their pleasure, their dancing and their music, their business and their anxieties, their politics and their troubles. Ignorant – willfully ignorant in many cases – and in other instances knowing all about the truth and not caring at all. But all of them, the whole mass of them, sweeping on and up in their blasphemies to the Throne of God. While my mind was thus engaged, I had a vision.

> **LIGHT from the BIBLE**
>
> *". . . snatch others from the fire and save them; to others show mercy, mixed with fear – hating even the clothing stained by corrupted flesh."*
>
> JUDE 23

Booth's vision

I saw a dark and stormy ocean. Over it the clouds hung heavily; through them every now and then vivid lightening flashed and loud thunder rolled, while the winds moaned, and the waves rose and foamed, towered and broke, only to rise and foam, tower and break again.

In that ocean I thought I saw myriads of poor human beings plunging and floating, shouting and shrieking, cursing and struggling and drowning; and as they cursed and screamed they rose and shrieked again, and then some sank to rise no more.

A mighty rock

And I saw out of this dark angry ocean, a mighty rock that rose up with its summit towering high above the clouds that overhung the stormy sea.

> ## Quotation to ponder
>
> *"The greatest task of the church is not solving political problems, nor is it to meet social needs but it is a renewed truthful proclamation of Jesus Christ as Lord."*
>
> JOHN R. W. STOTT

And all around the base of this great rock I saw a vast platform. Onto this platform, I saw with delight a number of the poor struggling, drowning wretches continually climbing out of the angry ocean. And I saw that a few of those who were already safe on the platform were helping the poor creatures still in the angry waters to reach the place of safety.

Rescuing the perishing

On looking more closely I found a number of those who had been rescued, industriously working and scheming by ladders, ropes, boats and other means more effective, to deliver the poor strugglers out of the sea. Here and there were some who actually jumped into the water, regardless of the consequences in their passion to "rescue the perishing." And I hardly know which gladdened me the most – the sight of the poor drowning people climbing onto the rocks reaching a place of safety, or the devotion and self-sacrifice of those whose whole being was wrapped up in the effort for their deliverance.

Short memories

As I looked on, I saw that the occupants of that platform were quite a mixed company. That is, they were divided into different "sets" or classes, and they occupied themselves with different pleasures and employments. But only a very few of them seemed to make it their business to get the people out of the sea.

But what puzzled me most was the fact that though all of them had been rescued at one time or another from the ocean, nearly everyone seemed to have

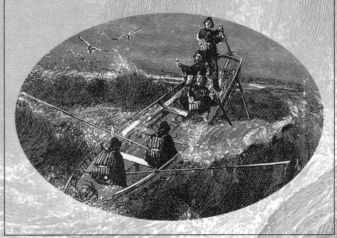

forgotten all about it. Anyway, it seemed the memory of its darkness and danger no longer troubled them at all. And what seemed equally strange and perplexing to me was that these people did not even seem to have any care – that is any agonizing care – about the poor perishing ones who were struggling and drowning right before their very eyes. Many of these people were their own husbands and wives, brothers and sisters and even their own children.

> **LIGHT** *from the* **BIBLE**
>
> *"I have made you a watchman for the house of Israel; so hear the word I speak and give them warning from me."*
>
> EZEKIEL 3:17

Quotation to ponder

"God is sovereign, of course, and can penetrate even the hardest heart with his Word. But we, as his instruments, are called to love people enough to reach out to them in their own language."

CHARLES COLSON

Astonishing unconcern

Now this astonishing unconcern could not have been the result of ignorance or lack of knowledge, because they lived right there in full sight of it all and even talked about it sometimes. Many even went regularly to hear lectures and sermons in which the awful state of these poor drowning creatures was described.

Absorbing activities

I have always said that the occupants of this platform were engaged in different pursuits and pastimes. Some of them were absorbed day and night in trading and business in order to make gain, storing up their savings in boxes, safes, and the like.

Many spent their time in amusing themselves with growing flowers on the side of the rock, others in painting pieces of cloth or in playing music, or in dressing themselves up in different styles and walking about to be admired. Some occupied themselves chiefly in eating and drinking, others were taken up with arguing about the poor drowning creatures that had already been rescued.

LIGHT from the BIBLE

"When I say to a wicked man, 'You will surely die,' and you do not warn him or speak out to dissuade him from his evil ways in order to save his life, that wicked man will die for his sin, and I will hold you accountable for his blood."

EZEKIEL 3:18

No care

But the thing to me that seemed the most amazing was that those on the platform to whom He called, who heard His voice and felt that they ought to obey it – at least they said they did – those who confessed to love Him much were in full sympathy with Him in the task He had undertaken – who worshiped Him or who professed to do so – were so taken up with their trades and professions, their money saving and pleasures, their families and circles, their religions and arguments about it, and their preparation for going to the mainland, that they did not listen to the cry that came to them from this Wonderful Being who had Himself gone down into the sea. Anyway, if they heard it they did not heed it. They did not care. And so the multitude went on right before them struggling and shrieking and drowning in the darkness.

Even stranger

And then I saw something that seemed to me even more strange than anything that had gone on before in this strange vision. I saw that some of these people on the platform whom this Wonderful Being had called to, wanting them to come and help Him in His difficult task of saving these perishing creatures, were always praying and crying out to Him to come to them!

Assurance sought

Some wanted Him to come and stay with them, and spend His time and strength in making them happier. Others wanted Him to come and take away various doubts and misgivings they had concerning the truth of

Quotation to ponder

"Religion is caught, not taught."

W. R. INGE

some letters He had written them. Some wanted Him to come and make them feel more secure on the rock – so secure that they would be quite sure that they should never slip off again into the ocean. Numbers of others wanted Him to make them feel quite certain that they would really get off the rock and onto the mainland someday: because as a matter of fact, it was well known that some had walked so carelessly as to lose their footing, and had fallen back again into the stormy waters.

> ### LIGHT *from the* BIBLE
>
> *"Jesus went through all the towns and villages, teaching in their synagogues, preaching the good news of the kingdom and healing every disease and sickness. When he saw the crowds, he had compassion on them, because they were harassed and helpless, like sheep without a shepherd. Then he said to his disciples, 'The harvest is plentiful but the workers are few.'"*
> MATTHEW 9:35-37

Unnecessary request

So these people used to meet and get up as high on the rock as they could, and looking toward the mainland (where they thought the Great Being was) they would cry out, "Come to us! Come and help us!" And all the while He was down (by His Spirit) among the poor struggling, drowning creatures in the angry deep, with His arms around them trying to drag them out, and looking up – oh! so longingly but all in vain – to those on the rock, crying to them with His voice all hoarse from calling, "Come to Me! Come, and help Me!

Obvious meaning

And then I understood it all. It was plain enough. The sea was the ocean of life – the sea of real, actual human existence. That lightning was the gleaming of piercing truth coming from Jehovah's Throne. That thunder was the distant

echoing of the wrath of God. Those multitudes of people shrieking, struggling, and agonizing in the stormy sea, was the thousands and thousands of poor harlots and harlot makers, of drunkards and drunkard makers, of thieves, liars, blasphemers, and ungodly people of every kindred, tongue, and nation.

Quotation to ponder

"The Church exists for nothing else but to draw men into Christ, to make them little Christs."

C. S. LEWIS

A terrible sea

Oh what a raging sea it was! And oh, what multitudes of rich and poor, ignorant and educated were there. They were all so unlike in their outward circumstances and conditions, yet all alike in one thing – all sinners before God – all held by, and holding onto, some iniquity, fascinated by some idol, the slaves of some devilish lust, and ruled by the foul fiend from the bottomless pit!

"All alike in one thing?" No, all alike in two things – not only the same in their wickedness but, unless rescued, the same in their sinking, sinking, down, down, down, to the same terrible doom.

That great sheltering rock represented Calvary, the place where Jesus had died for them. And the people on it were those who had been rescued. The way they used their energies, gifts, and time represented the occupations and amusements of those who professed to be saved from sin and hell – followers of the Lord Jesus Christ.

The handful of fierce, determined ones, who were risking their own lives in saving the perishing were true soldiers of the cross of Jesus.

That Mighty Being who was calling to them from the midst of the angry waters was the Son of God, "the same yesterday, today and forever" who is still struggling and interceding to save the dying multitudes about us from this terrible doom of damnation, and whose voice can be heard above the music, machinery, and noise of life, calling on the rescued to come and help Him save the world.

> **LIGHT** *from the* **BIBLE**
>
> *"After this the Lord appointed seventy-two others and sent them two by two ahead of him to every town and place where he was about to go."*
>
> LUKE 10:1

A young Christian

A young Christian once came to me, and told me that for some time she had been giving the Lord her profession and prayers and money, but now she wanted to give Him her life.

She wanted to go right into the fight. In other words, she wanted to go to His assistance in the sea.

William Booth

Quotation to ponder

"My friends in Christ, you are rescued from the waters, you are on the rock, He is in the dark sea calling on you to come to Him and help Him. Will you go? Look for yourselves. The surging sea of life, crowded with perishing multitudes rolls up to the very spot on which you stand."

WILLIAM BOOTH

— *Part 3* —
STORIES *illuminating*
BIBLE VERSES

The art collector

Father and son art collectors

A wealthy man and his son loved to collect rare works of art. They had everything in their collection, from Picasso to Raphael. They would often sit together and admire the great works of art.

The most prized portrait

When the Vietnam conflict broke out, the son went to war. He was very courageous and died in battle while rescuing another soldier. The father was notified and grieved deeply for his only son. About a month later, just before Christmas, there was a knock at the door.

A young man stood at the door with a large package in his hands. He said, "Sir, you don't know me, but I am the soldier for whom your son gave his life. He saved many lives that day, and he was carrying me to safety when a bullet struck him in the heart and he died instantly. He often talked about you, and your love for art."

The young man held out this package. "I know this isn't much. I'm not really a great artist, but I think your son would have wanted you to have this." The father opened the package. It was a portrait of his son, painted by the young man. He stared in awe at the way the soldier had captured the personality of his son in the painting. The father was so drawn to the eyes that his own eyes welled up with tears. He thanked the young man and offered to pay him for the picture. "Oh, no sir, I could never repay what your son did for me. It's a gift," insisted the young man.

The father hung the portrait over his mantle. Every time visitors came to his home he took them to see the portrait of his son before he showed them any of the other great works he had collected.

LIGHT *from the* BIBLE

"For God so loved the world that he gave his one and only Son . . . For God did not send his Son into the world to condemn the world, but to save the world through him. Whoever believes in him is not condemned, but whoever does not believe stands condemned already because he has not believed in the name of God's one and only Son."

JOHN 3:16-18

A strange auction

The man died a few months later. There was to be a great auction of his paintings. Many influential people gathered, excited over seeing the great paintings and

LIGHT *from the* **BIBLE**

"He who has the Son has life."

1 JOHN 5:12

having an opportunity to purchase one for their collection. On the platform sat the painting of the son. The auctioneer pounded his gavel.

"We will start the bidding with this picture of the son. Who will bid for this picture?" There was silence. Then a voice in the back of the room shouted, "We want to see the famous paintings. Skip this one." But the auctioneer persisted. "Will someone bid for this painting? Who will start the bidding? $100, $200?" Another voice shouted angrily: "We didn't come to see this painting. We came to see the Van Goghs, the Rembrandts. Get on with the real bids!"

"Who will take the son?"

But still the auctioneer continued. "The son! The son! Who'll take the son?"
Finally, a voice came from the very back of the room. It was the longtime gardener of the man and his son. "I'll give $10 for the painting." Being a poor man, it was all he could afford.

"We have $10, who will bid $20?"

"Give it to him for $10. Let's see the masters," someone shouted.

"$10 is the bid, won't someone bid $20?" The crowd was becoming angry. They didn't want the picture of the son. They wanted the more worthy investments for their collections. The auctioneer pounded the gavel. "Going once, twice, SOLD for $10!"

End of the auction

A man sitting on the second row shouted, "Now let's get on with the collection!"

The auctioneer laid down his gavel. "I'm sorry, the auction's over."

"What about the paintings?" came the cries from the floor.

"I am sorry. When I was called to conduct this auction, I was told of a secret stipulation in the will. I was not allowed to reveal that stipulation until this time. Only the painting of the son would be auctioned. Whoever bought that painting would inherit the entire estate, including the paintings. The man who took the son gets everything!"

Quotation to ponder

"For though God's love is indeed unconditional, his acceptance of us is not, since it depends on our repentance and our faith in Jesus Christ."

JOHN R.W. STOTT

The widow's lakhs

Gandhi's collection

Mahatma Gandhi went from city to city, village to village, collecting funds for the Charkha Sangh, a welfare organization founded by Gandhi.

LIGHT *from the* BIBLE

"Jesus sat down opposite the place where the offerings were put and watched the crowd putting their money into the temple treasury. Many rich people threw in large amounts. But a poor widow came and put in two very small copper coins, worth only a fraction of a penny. Calling his disciples to him, Jesus said, 'I tell you the truth, this poor widow has put more into the treasury than all the others. They all gave out of their wealth; but she, out of her poverty, put in everything – all she had to live on.'"

MARK 12:41-44

During one of his tours he addressed a meeting in Orissa. After his speech a poor old woman got up. She was bent with age, her hair was gray and her clothes were in tatters. The volunteers tried to stop her, but she fought her way to the place where Gandhi was sitting. "I must see him," she insisted and going up to Gandhi touched his feet.

The treasurer

Then from the folds of her sari she brought out a copper coin and placed it at his feet. Gandhi picked up the copper coin and put it away carefully. The Charkha Sangh funds

Quotation to ponder

"If our expenditure on comforts, luxuries, amusements, etc., is up to the standard common among those with the same income as our own, we are probably giving away too little. If our charities do not at all pinch or hamper us, I should say they are too small. There ought to be things we should like to do and cannot because our charitable expenditure excludes them."

C. S. LEWIS

were looked after by Jamnalal Bajaj. He asked Gandhi for the coin but Gandhi refused. "I keep checks worth thousands of rupees for the Charkha Sangh," Jamnalal Bajaj said laughingly "yet you won't trust me with a copper coin."

"This copper coin is worth much more than those thousands," Gandhi said. "If a man has several lakhs and he gives away a thousand or two, it doesn't mean much. But this coin was perhaps all that the poor woman possessed. She gave me all she had. That was very generous of her. What a great sacrifice she made. That is why I value this copper coin more than a crore (ten million) of rupees."

The priceless pearl

Diving for pearls

A heavy splash was followed by many ripples and then the water below the pier was still. An American missionary crouched on the low Indian pier, his eyes riveted on the place where a stream of little bubbles rose to the surface from deep under the water. Suddenly a head appeared and a pair of bright eyes looked up. Then the old Indian pearl diver was clambering onto the dock, grinning and shaking the water from his shining oiled body.

The best pearl?

"As nice a dive as I've ever seen, Rambhau!" cried David Morse, the American missionary.

"Look at this one, Sahib," said Rambhau, taking a big oyster from between his teeth. "I think it'll be good."

> **LIGHT *from the* BIBLE**
>
> *"Again, the kingdom of heaven is like a merchant looking for fine pearls. When he found one of great value, he went away and sold everything he had and bought it."*
>
> MATTHEW 13:45-46

Morse took it and while he was prying it open with his pocketknife Rambhau was pulling other small oysters from his loincloth. "Rambhau! Look!" exclaimed Morse, "Why, it's a treasure!"

"Yes, a good one," shrugged the diver.

"Good! Have you ever seen a better pearl? It's

perfect, isn't it?" Morse had been turning the big pearl over and over and then handed it to the Indian.

Not a perfect pearl

"Oh, yes, there are better pearls, much better. Why, I have one . . . " his voice trailed off. "See this one – the imperfections – the black specks here, this tiny dent; even in shape it is a bit oblong, but good as pearls go. It is just as you say of your God. To themselves people look perfect, but God sees them as they actually are."

The two men started up the dusty road to town.

> *Quotation to ponder*
>
> *"Until people feel that they owe everything to God, that they are protected by his fatherly care and that he is the author of all their blessings, so that nothing should be sought apart from him, they will never submit to him voluntarily."*
>
> JOHN CALVIN

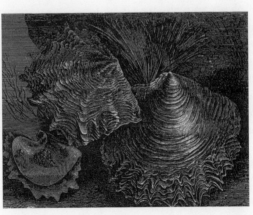

Too easy

"You're right, Rambhau. And God offers a perfect righteousness to all who will simply believe and accept His free offer of salvation through His Beloved Son."

"But, Sahib, as so many times before I have told you, it's too easy. I cannot accept that. Perhaps I am too proud. I must work for my place in heaven."

One way to heaven

"Oh, Rambhau! Don't you see, you'll never get to heaven that way. There's only one way to heaven. And see, Rambhau, you are getting older now. Perhaps this is your last season of diving for pearls.

"If you ever want to see heaven's gates of pearl, you must accept the new life God offers you in His Son."

"My last season! Yes, you are right. Today was my last day of diving. This is the last month of the year; and I have preparations to make."

My pilgrimage

"You should prepare for the life to come."

"That's just what I'm going to do. Do you see that man over there? He is a pilgrim, perhaps to Bombay or Calcutta. He walks barefooted and picks the sharpest stones and see – every few rods he kneels down and kisses the road. That is good. The first day of the New Year I begin my pilgrimage. All my life I have planned it. I shall make sure of heaven this time. I am going to Delhi on my knees."

"Man! You're crazy! It's more than fourteen hundred miles to Delhi! The skin will break on your knees, and you'll have blood poisoning or leprosy before you get to Bombay."

"No, I must get to Delhi. And then the immortals will reward me. The suffering will be sweet, for it will purchase heaven for me."

Free salvation too easy

"Rambhau! My friend! You can't! How can I let you do this when Jesus Christ has died to purchase heaven for you?" But the old man could not be moved.

Quotation to ponder

"If you are trying to be a Christian, it is a sure sign you are not one."

OSWALD CHAMBERS

"You are my dearest friend on earth, Sahib Morse. Through all these years you have stood beside me. In sickness and want you have been sometimes my only friend. But even you cannot turn me from this great desire to purchase eternal bliss. I must go to Delhi." It was

> **LIGHT** *from the* **BIBLE**
>
> *"But because of his great love for us, God, who is rich in mercy, made us alive with Christ even when we were dead in transgressions – it is by grace you have been saved."*
>
> EPHESIANS 2:4-5

useless. The old pearl diver could not understand, could not accept the free salvation of Christ.

The invitation

One afternoon Morse answered a knock at the door to find Rambhau there. "My good friend!" cried Morse. "Come in, Rambhau."

"No," said the pearl diver, "I want you to come with me to my house, Sahib, for a short time. I have something to show you. Please do not say, 'No.'"

The heart of the missionary leaped. Perhaps God was answering prayer at last. "Of course, I'll come," he said.

"I leave for Delhi just one week from today, you know," said Rambhau as they neared his house ten minutes later. The missionary's heart sank. Morse was seated on the chair his friend had built especially for him, where many times he had sat explaining to the diver God's way to heaven.

Rambhau's son

Rambhau left the room to return soon with a small but heavy English strong box. "I have had this box for years," he said. "I keep only one thing in it. Now I will tell you about it. Sahib Morse, I once had a son."

"A son! Why, Rambhau, you had never said a word about him!"

"No, Sahib, I couldn't." Even as he spoke the diver's eyes were moistened. "Now, I must tell you, for soon I will leave, and who knows whether I shall ever return? My son was a diver, too. He was the best pearl diver on the coast of India. He had the swiftest dive, the keenest eye, the strongest arm, the longest breath of any man who sought for pearls. What joy he brought me! He always dreamed of finding a pearl beyond all that had ever been found. One day he found it. But when he found it, he had already been underwater too long. He lost his life soon after."

> *Quotation to ponder*
>
> "There is the sun; I do not know how many thousands of times the sun is bigger than the earth, and yet the sun can come into a little room, and what is more, the sun can get in through a chink. So Christ can come in through a little faith, a mere chink of confidence."
>
> C. H. SPURGEON

LIGHT *from the* BIBLE

"He came to that which was his own, but his own did not receive him. Yet to all who received him, to those who believed in his name, he gave the right to become children of God – children born not of natural descent, nor of human decision or a husband's will, but born of God. The Word became flesh and made his dwelling among us. We have seen his glory, the glory of the One and Only, who came from the Father, full of grace and truth."

JOHN 1:11-14

"Accept my pearl"

The old pearl diver bowed his head and for a moment his whole body shook. "All these years I have kept the pearl," he continued, "but now I am going, not to return... and to you, my best friend, I am giving my pearl." The old man worked the combination on the strong box and drew from it a carefully wrapped package. Gently opening the cotton, he picked up a mammoth pearl and placed it in the hand of the missionary. It was one of the largest pearls ever found off the coast of India, and it glowed with a luster and brilliance never seen in cultured pearls. It would have brought a fabulous sum in any market.

For a moment the missionary was speechless and gazed with awe.

"Rambhau," he said, "this is a wonderful pearl, an amazing pearl. Let me buy it. I would give ten thousand rupees for it."

"Sahib," said Rambhau, stiffening his whole body, "this pearl is beyond all price. No man in all the world has money enough to pay what this pearl is worth to me. On the market a million rupees could not buy it. I will not sell it. You may only have it as a gift."

Priceless pearl refused

"No, Rambhau, I cannot accept that. As much as I want the pearl, I cannot accept it that way. Perhaps I am proud, but that is too easy. I must pay for it, or work for it."

"Just accept it"

The old pearl diver was stunned. "You don't understand at all, Sahib. Don't you see? My only son gave his life to get this pearl, and I wouldn't sell it for any money. Its worth is in the lifeblood of my son. I cannot sell this, but do permit me to give it to you. Just accept it in token of the love I bear for you."

Acted-out parable

The missionary was choked and for a moment could not speak. Then he

Quotation to ponder

"Christ will not compel you. He doesn't force His way into anybody's life. He stands and knocks at your heart's door and asks you to open the door. You can say no to Christ. You can shake your fist at Him if you want to and there's nothing He can do about it, because He gave you a will of your own. It's a matter of personal choice."

BILLY GRAHAM

gripped the hand of the old man. "Rambhau," he said in a low voice, "don't you see? That is just what you have been saying to God." The diver looked long and searchingly at the missionary and slowly he began to understand.

"God is offering to you eternal life as a free gift. It is so great and priceless that no man on earth could buy it. No man on earth could earn it. No man is good enough to deserve it. It cost God the lifeblood of His only Son to make entrance for you into heaven. In a hundred pilgrimages, you could not earn that entrance. All you can do is accept it as a token of God's love for you, a sinner. Rambhau, of course, I will accept the pearl in deep humility, praying God I may be worthy of your love. Rambhau, won't you too accept God's great gift of eternal life, in deep humility, knowing it cost Him the death of His Son to offer it to you? 'The gift of God is eternal life through Jesus Christ our Lord.'"

Acceptance

Great tears were rolling down the cheeks of the old man. The veil was lifting. He understood at last. "Sahib, I see it now. I believe Jesus gave Himself for me. I accept Him."

Quotation to ponder

"To the question; what does it mean to believe on the Lord Jesus Christ? the old gospel replies; it means knowing oneself to be a sinner, and Christ to have died for sinners; abandoning all self-righteousness and self-confidence, and casting oneself wholly upon Him for pardon and peace; and exchanging one's natural enmity and rebellion against God for a spirit of grateful submission to the will of Christ through the renewing of one's heart by the Holy Ghost."

J. I. PACKER

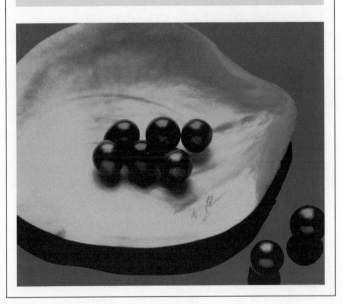

Four wives

O nce upon a time there was a rich king who had
four wives

> ### LIGHT from the BIBLE
>
> *"Then he said to them all: 'If anyone would come after me, he must deny himself and take up his cross daily and follow me. For whoever wants to save his life will lose it, but whoever loses his life for me will save it. What good is it for a man to gain the whole world, and yet lose or forfeit his very self?'"*
>
> LUKE 9:23-25

The fourth wife

He loved the fourth wife the most and adorned her with rich robes and treated her to the finest delicacies. He gave her nothing but the best.

The third wife

He also loved his third wife very much and was always showing her off to neighboring kingdoms. However, he feared that one day she would leave him for another.

The second wife

He also loved his second wife. She was his confidant and was always kind, considerate, and patient with him. Whenever the king faced a problem he could confide in her and she would help him get through the difficult times.

Quotation to ponder

"Whoever will labor to get rid of self, to deny himself according to the instructions of Christ, strikes at once at the root of every evil, and finds the germ of every good."

FRANÇOIS FÉNELON

The first wife

The king's first wife was a very loyal partner and had made great contributions in maintaining his wealth and kingdom. However, he did not love the first wife. Although she loved him deeply he hardly ever noticed her.

The dying king

One day the king fell ill and he knew his time was short. He thought of his luxurious life and wondered, "I now have four wives with me, but when I die, I'll be all alone."

Thus, he asked the fourth wife, "I have loved you the most, endowed you with the finest clothing, and showered great care over you. Now that I am dying, will you follow me and keep me company?"

"No way!" replied the fourth wife and she walked away without another word. Her answer cut like a sharp knife right into his heart.

The sad king then asked his third wife, "I have loved you all my life.

> **LIGHT** *from the* **BIBLE**
>
> *"Then he told them many things in parables, saying: 'A farmer went out to sow his seed . . . Other seed fell among thorns, which grew up and choked the plants . . . The one who received the seed that fell among the thorns is the man who hears the word, but the worries of this life and the deceitfulness of wealth choke it, making it unfruitful.'"*
>
> MATTHEW 13:3,7,22

Now that I'm dying will you follow me and keep me company?"

"No!" she replied. "Life is too good! When you die, I am going to remarry!" His heart sank and turned cold.

He the king asked the second wife, "I have always turned to you for help and you've always been there for me. When I die will you follow me and keep me company?"

"I'm sorry, I can't help you out this time!" replied the second wife. "At the very most, I can send you to your grave." Her answer came like a bolt of lightning, and the king was devastated.

An unexpected voice

Then a voice called out: "I'll leave with you and follow you no matter where you go."

The king looked up, and there was his first wife. She was so skinny as she suffered from malnutrition and neglect. Greatly grieved, the king said, "I should have taken better care of you when I had the chance!"

Explanation

In reality, we all have four wives in our lives.

Our fourth wife is our body. No matter how much time and effort we lavish in making it look good, it will leave us when we die.

Our third wife is our possessions, status, and wealth. When we die, it will all go to others.

Our second wife is our family and friends. No matter how much they have been there for us, the furthest they can stay by us is up to the grave.

And our first wife is our Soul. Often neglected in pursuit of wealth, power, and pleasures of the world. However, our Soul is the only thing that will follow us wherever we go. It is the only part of us who will follow us to the throne of God and continue with us throughout eternity.

Quotation to ponder

"Man should not consider his outward possessions as his own, but as common to all, so as to share them without hesitation when others are in need."

THOMAS AQUINAS

The wooden bowl

The ailing grandfather

A frail old man went to live with his son, daughter-in-law, and four-year-old grandson. The old man's hands trembled, his eyesight was blurred, and his step faltered.

The family ate together at the table. But the elderly grandfather's shaky hands and failing sight made eating difficult. Peas rolled off his spoon onto the floor. When he grasped the glass, milk spilled on the tablecloth.

LIGHT *from the* **BIBLE**

"If anyone does not provide for his relatives, and especially for his immediate family, he has denied the faith and is worse than an unbeliever."

1 TIMOTHY 5:8

Put in the corner

The son and daughter-in-law became irritated with the mess. "We must do something about Grandfather," said the son. I've had enough of his spilled milk, noisy eating, and food on the floor. So the husband and wife set a small table in the corner. There, Grandfather ate alone while the rest of the family enjoyed dinner. Since Grandfather had broken a dish or two, his food was served in a wooden bowl.

When the family glanced in Grandfather's direction, sometimes he had a tear in his eye as he sat alone.

Still, the only words the couple had for him were sharp admonitions when he dropped a fork or spilled food.

The kind grandson

The four-year-old watched it all in silence. One evening before supper, the father noticed his son playing with wood scraps on the floor. He asked the child sweetly, "What are you making?"

Just as sweetly, the boy responded, "Oh, I am making a little bowl for you and Mama to eat your food when I grow up." The four-year-old smiled and went back to work.

Tears

The words so struck the parents that they were speechless. Then tears started to stream down their cheeks. Though no word was spoken, both knew what must be done. That evening the husband took Grandfather's hand and gently led him back to the family table. For the remainder of his days he ate every meal with the family. And for some reason, neither husband nor wife seemed to care any longer when a fork was dropped, milk spilled, or the tablecloth soiled.

Quotation to ponder

"Let our compassion be a mirror where we may see in ourselves that likeness and that true image which belong to the Divine nature and Divine essence."

ISAAC OF SYRIA

Alexander Fleming

To the rescue

His name was Fleming, and he was a poor Scottish farmer. One day, while trying to eke out a living for his family, he heard a cry for help coming from a nearby bog. He dropped his tools and ran to the bog. There, mired to his waist in black muck, was a terrified boy, screaming and struggling to free himself. Farmer Fleming saved the lad from what could have been a slow and terrifying death.

LIGHT *from the* BIBLE

"What good is it, my brothers, if a man claims to have faith but has no deeds? Can such faith save him? Suppose a brother or sister is without clothes and daily food. If one of you says to him, 'Go, I wish you well; keep warm and well fed,' but does nothing about his physical needs, what good is it? In the same way, faith by itself, if it is not accompanied by action, is dead."

JAMES 2:14-17

An education

The next day, a fancy carriage pulled up to the Scotsman's sparse surroundings. An elegantly dressed nobleman stepped out and introduced himself as the father of the boy Farmer Fleming had saved. "I want to repay you," said the nobleman. "You saved my son's life."

"No, I can't accept payment for what I did," the Scottish farmer replied, waving off the offer. At that moment, the

Quotation to ponder

*"Faith cannot help doing good works constantly.
It doesn't stop to ask if good works ought to be done,
but before anyone asks, it already has done them
and continues to do them without ceasing. Anyone
who does not do good works in this manner is
an unbeliever."*

MARTIN LUTHER

farmer's own son came to the door of the family hovel.
"Is that your son?" the nobleman asked.
"Yes," the farmer replied proudly.
"I'll make you a deal. Let me take him and give him a
good education. If the lad is anything like his father,
he'll grow to a man you can be proud of."

Dr. Fleming
And that he did. In time, Farmer Fleming's son
graduated from St. Mary's Hospital Medical School in
London, and went on to become known throughout the
world as the noted Sir Alexander Fleming, the
discoverer of penicillin.

Postscript
Years afterward, the nobleman's son was stricken with
pneumonia. What saved him? Penicillin.
The name of the nobleman? Lord Randolph Churchill.
His son's name? Sir Winston Churchill.

The complaining monk

Two words a year

A man joined a monastery where the monks were only allowed to speak two words a year, and those to the abbot. At the end of each year they were given an audience and said their two words. Naturally they were expected to be something along the lines of "Jesus loves" or some other eternal verity.

However, at the end of his first year the novice offered, "Bed hard" and at the end of the second year, "Food bad" and at the end of the third year his two words were, "I quit."

"I'm not surprised," said the abbot, "you've done nothing but whine ever since you came here."

LIGHT *from the* BIBLE

"I have learned to be content whatever the circumstances. I know what it is to be in need, and I know what it is to have plenty. I have learned the secret of being content in any and every situation, whether well fed or hungry, whether living in plenty or in want."

PHILIPPIANS 4:11-12

Quotation to ponder

"Nobody who gets enough food and clothing in a world where most are hungry and cold has any business to talk about 'misery.'"

C. S. LEWIS